TREASURES

NORWICH

Edited by Steve Twelvetree

First published in Great Britain in 2002 by
YOUNG WRITERS
Remus House,
Coltsfoot Drive,
Peterborough, PE2 9JX
Telephone (01733) 890066

HB ISBN 0 75433 832 0
SB ISBN 0 75433 833 9

FOREWORD

This year, the Young Writers' Hidden Treasures competition proudly presents a showcase of the best poetic talent from over 72,000 up-and-coming writers nationwide.

Young Writers was established in 1991 and we are still successful, even in today's technologically-led world, in promoting and encouraging the reading and writing of poetry.

The thought, effort, imagination and hard work put into each poem impressed us all, and once again, the task of selecting poems was a difficult one, but nevertheless, an enjoyable experience.

We hope you are as pleased as we are with the final selection and that you and your family continue to be entertained with *Hidden Treasures Norwich* for many years to come.

CONTENTS

Heartsease Middle School

Victoria Crisp	58
Jack Ives-Keeler	59
Ethan Holloway	60
Ebony Dawson	61
Sally Hartle	61
Sharna Wright	62
Sarah Wilson	62
Michael Britt	63
Rebecca Jeary	64
Leanne Hannant	64
Jasmine Brown	65
Perrie Greaves	65
Natasha Burns	65
Martin Westgate	66
Max Banfield	66
Joshua Hoy	67
Lauren Bridge	67
Sam Durrant	68
Roxanne Kelf	69
Emma Stone	70
Emma Joy	70
Stevie Louise Childs	71
Dayna Bobby	71
Olivia Lince-Andrade	72
Sean Hankins	72
Arran Starling	73
Sophie Young & Heloise Bush	73
Natalie Curran	74
Samantha Jones	74
Nathan Sadd	75
Melissa Moore	75
Danielle Wright	76
Aimée Edwards	77
Helen Middleton	78
Sarah Snowling	78
Josh Starr	79
Leighann Cox	79

Sophie Slatter	80
Matthew Asker	80
Suzanne Breeze	81
Aaron Curran	81
Daniel Seely	82
Stevie Howes	82
Kelsey Gooda	83
Jessica Robinson	83
Curtis Pointin	84
Gavin Marrison	84
Jordan Wood	85
Emma Carway	85
Gabby Timbers	86
Jack Murphy	86
Daniel Ribera	87
Kyle Wright	87
Jacqueline Pasco	88
Samantha Cox	88
Lauren Aldis	89
Olivia Davison-George	89
Charmaine King	90
Kirsha Harding	90
Kirsty Anne Burns	91
Nathaniel Brian Richard Harper	91
Michael Hubbard	92

Kenninghall Primary School

James Nicholls	93
Thomas Brown	93
Joshua Bailey	94
Torr Cumming	94
Sophie Cumming	95
Paul Coomber	95
Katie Pavid	96
Robbie Goodsell	96
Marcus Searle	97
Jack Burrows	98
Glenn Stolash	98

Danielle Shaw	99
Aaron Grime	99
Sophie Fuller	100
Summer Copeland	100
Hayley Brown	101
Laura Turner	101
Ashton Flounders	102
Lewis Weatherburn	102
Ben Garwood	103
George Nicholls	103
Lewis Knights	104

Mulbarton Middle School

Jenna Clarke-Frary	104
Sam Thelwell	105
Sophie Bland	105
Emma Traynor	106
Emily Peacock	106
Jessica Ballard	107
Molly Gallant	108
Holly Hunter	108
Jamie Allison	109
Ralph Moore	110
Abbey King	110
Luke Ashby	111
Hannah Marriott	112
Megan Cletheroe	112
Chris Willimott	113
Bethany Wyer	114
Shane Barrett	114
Nick Mackenzie	115
Amy Jacobs	115
Jessica Davey	116
Juliette Samson	116
Cayce Curtis	117
Hayley Jane Parker	118
Rebecca Willis	118
Cherry Meredith	119

Saxlingham Primary School

James Chadwick	155
Alfie Chapman	155
Alice Stockton	156
Kimberley Betts	156
Joshua Tovée	157
Freya Lincoln	157
Sophie Jolliffe	158
Joshua Smith	159
Abigail Burrell	160
Hollie Allison	160

Sprowston Middle School

Marcus Fenn	160
James Slater	161
Megan Lythgoe	161
Conor Ferguson	162
Blaine Kenneally	162
Rachael Dixon	163
Thomas Whitehouse	163
Freya Riseborough	164
Andrew Godfrey	164
Louise Daynes	165
Tayalor Gribben	166
Lewis Colman	166
Amy Watts	167
Samantha Ellis	167
Pinku Raja	168
Karlie Aldous	168
Connor Tooke	169
Mitchell Turner	169
Kirsty Copping	170
Alix Pudwell	170
Emma Minns	171
Jamie Steven Brown	172
Emma Lant	172
Daniel L Knights	173
Chelsey Ryder	174
Eleanor Slater	175

The Poems

FIREMAN

I am a fireman, fellow
I have a hat that is yellow
I am so strong
And I am long, I am a fireman, fellow.

I am a fireman, fellow
I have a coat that is yellow
I am so brave
People's lives I save, I am a fireman, fellow.

I am a fireman, fellow
I have a pair of shoes that are yellow
People sometimes die,
But their friends say goodbye
I am a fireman, fellow.

I am a fireman, fellow
I have a pair of gloves that are yellow
I am so happy if people are still alive
And they are surprised that I am a fireman, fellow.

Maria Gardikiotis (9)

DREAMTIME

D   uring the mists of time
R   ainbow Serpent created the universe
E   very animal tribe is born from her
A   ll have a totem they know and respect
M   any ate their sacred animal
T   o them their lives were set in stone
I   t was human life for those who kept the promise
M   oonlight cast upon on the stones, rocks and mountains to remind
E   veryone to keep the promise of the Rainbow Serpent.

Kirsty Hinde (11)

GONE

When you left you broke my heart
And I will never understand why we have to be apart
Not even remembering you can ease the pain
Because nothing can bring you back again.

Even though you were left in peace
I still don't think about you with ease
You lived life to the top and full,
But all I have is memories of you.

Now without you I am not worth living
You must have been the best human being
Now you are gone I am left on my own
We went together like dog and bone
        And now you are gone.

Lauren Aimee Matthews (11)
Acle St Edmund Primary School

SUMMER

The summer holidays are really cool
Six whole weeks without going to school
Days out and picnics are really fun
Running on the beach and playing in the sun
No homework, spellings or tables to do
But fun things like a trip to the zoo
Lazy hours spent in the garden with mates
Camping trips, eating meals off paper plates
Swimming, walking or riding your bike
Are the sort of things that I like.

Laura Bould (10)
Acle St Edmund Primary School

ANIMAL NAME POEM

The dog named Jock
Wore a frock
The hamster called Jack
Bit my back
The other hamster called Buster
Held some oranges in a cluster
The cat called Yum
Scratched his tum
Pig named Lose
Picked his nose
The horse called Lance
Licked my pants
The other pig called Stig
Wore a wig!

Rhiannon White (9)
Acle St Edmund Primary School

THE SOLAR SYSTEM

The sun, the sun, the biggest of the lot
Then there's Mercury, it's very, very hot
Venus, Venus is made of gas
Earth has people, they all have a mass
Could there be aliens all over Mars?
Jupiter, Jupiter has got no cars
Saturn has got some beautiful rings
Uranus hasn't got any bees that sting
Could Neptune have an underground train?
I don't know but Pluto *stinks* of methane
Phew, that's the lot.

Daniel Hargrave (9)
Acle St Edmund Primary School

WE'RE LATE FOR SCHOOL

Hey, look at the time, it's half-past nine
We're late for school and that's the rule
It's half-past nine!

We're waiting in a line, having a great time
Hey, look at the time it's half-past nine
We're late for school but sometimes that's the only rule!

My mum and dad are absolutely mad
Because I'm late for school and that's the rule
My head is dead, that's why we're waiting in the line
We're having a great time, that's why it's half-past nine
And were late for school, that the new rule!

Victoria Hemmingway (9)
Acle St Edmund Primary School

RATS

Rats, rats
Get chased by cats
Who get hurt by bats

The rats are mean
When you have seen
Them eating a bean

Bats are scary
They're big and hairy
They make the cats go quite lairy

The cats we find
They can't make up their mind
So you be soft and kind.

Hannah Withers (9)
Acle St Edmund Primary School

BUMP

You are tucked up in bed fast asleep
And when dark comes
Strange things creep

But steady your nerves, don't take fright
When things go bump in the night

Ghouls empty your toy box, they try on your clothes
And tie up your teddy in pink satin bows

But steady your nerves, don't take fright
When things go bump in the night

For night-time's the time when spooks like to play
At first sight of sunlight they hurry away

So steady your nerves, don't take fright
When things go bump in the night.

Nicolle Shergold (10)
Acle St Edmund Primary School

RAIN

Rain, rain is insane
Rain, rain down the windowpane

Quick, quick close the door
Quick, quick it's on the floor

The rain will fall
The rain will flood the hall

The rain will die
Friends say 'Hi.'

Peter Wright (10)
Acle St Edmund Primary School

THE BIG STICKY CAKE

I'm feeling hungry,
What shall I make?
Perhaps I could cook
A *big* sticky cake!

Let's start with the butter
And add all the flour,
Put in the sugar
And stir for an hour.

Mix in some syrup,
A dollop of jam,
A whole tube of Smarties
And wafer-thin ham.

Hot melted chocolate,
Honey (one spoon),
Pop into the oven,
Be ready quite soon.

Mum come and look,
At this wonderful sight!
It smells rather yummy,
So please have a bite.

(Hmmm. Not sure about the ham!)

Ben Rumsey (10)
Acle St Edmund Primary School

LIONS

Lions, lions
Have a fluffy mane

No other animal
Has the same

The lion
Is the king of beasts

No one would dare
To walk near the King's lair.

Rosie Doroba (9)
Acle St Edmund Primary School

CATS

Some cats are fat,
Some cats are thin,
Some cats stay out,
Some cats stay in.

Some cats eat fish,
Some cats eat meats,
Some cats eat biscuits,
Some cats eat treats.

Some cats are happy,
Some cats are sad,
Some cats are naughty,
Some cats are bad.

Some people like cats,
Some people like dogs,
Some people like rabbits,
Some people like frogs.

But my cat is ginger,
And she loves me.

Katie Peck (11)
Acle St Edmund Primary School

MY SHADY FRIEND

Who is this?
She follows me everywhere I go.
I am fed up with her.
She is capricious.
She is black and shady and I do not like her one bit.
Sometimes she is a real copycat
And she only comes out when the sun comes out.

She can be fun when I am lonely.
I wonder if she likes me. I like her a lot.
I wonder if she is magic. I can't ask her
Because I have upset her. She will get over it.

She follows me every day.
She plays with me, but she does not play inside.

We love each other.

Lauren Taylor (9)
Acle St Edmund Primary School

CRASH! SLASH! BUMP! SMASH!

Crash! goes the rat
Crash! goes the cat
Slash! goes the rug
Slash! goes the curtain
Bump! goes the head
Bump! goes my leg
Smash! goes the vase
Smash! goes the plate
As you can see it is quite a hectic house.

Annabel Ellson (9)
Acle St Edmund Primary School

THE BOBLIN

Beware! The Boblin, evil and scary,
Bulging eyes and extremely hairy.
Away in a cave this creature dwells,
Amongst the rats and the terrible smells.

The Boblin's cave is cold and damp,
Along the tunnels you can hear him stamp.
The grimy walls are slowly dripping,
Whilst the murky slime is slowly slipping.

In the cave at the very core,
Corpses lie rotten and raw.
He pounds his victims until they're dead,
And eats them all from foot to head.

Even if you're bold and brave,
Beware, the Boblin and his cave.
So when you enter into the gloom,
Just remember you're destined for doom.

Simon Dowsett (9)
Acle St Edmund Primary School

RAIN

Rain, rain drives us insane,
Running down the windowpane,
Quick, quick close the door,
Too late, it's flooding the floor,
Not again,
Rain, rain drives me insane . . .

Graham Hart (9)
Acle St Edmund Primary School

THE CUB ON THE STAGE

Once there was a cub
Who went to the Gang Show
He had a really good time
And he nearly stole the show!

The headmaster was very pleased
And so were the pupils who came
To see the young man on stage
Doing the show for real!

For doing so well on the night
The school praised him
And along with his fellow performers
He was happy to accept the applause!

Stephen Brighton (10)
Acle St Edmund Primary School

MARS

If I was an astronaut
And visited Mars,
I'd climb in my spaceship
And stare at the stars.

I'd put on my spacesuit
It's cold on Mars,
I'd pick up some red dust
And put it in jars.

I'd take it home
To show everyone,
To prove I had been
To the planet fourth from the sun.

Lauren Hammond (10)
Acle St Edmund Primary School

WISHFUL THINKING

If I could have a wish come true,
This is what I'd like to do,
Become a famous football star,
And drive around in my flash car.

Every night I pray and pray,
To have the chance to finally play,
With Man United I'd be the best,
Wearing the number 7 vest.

My hero's name is Paul Scholes,
And just like him I'd score the goals,
A hat-trick is my aspiration,
Imagine all the adoration!

I know I'd love the crowd to roar,
Wanting me to score some more,
That is what I'd like to do,
If I could have a wish come true.

Ben Lewins (9)
Acle St Edmund Primary School

DOGGY

Doggy sit
Doggy lick
Doggy do a forward flip
Doggy stand
Doggy stay
Doggy lay
Doggy play.

Natalie Hodgson (9)
Acle St Edmund Primary School

GRYAFFIDON THE TERRIBLE

Gryaffidon the Terrible at
Number 666,
If he cannot kill you at first try,
He'll use sly tricks.

All the plans he hatches up
Are filled with destruction and kill,
To the ones who said, 'You'd never dare!'
He said, 'Oh yes I will!'

Gryaffidon the Terrible,
Grinadagar's his heir,
Grinadagar's as sly as a fox
And strong as a full grown bear.

End of a rule of terror,
End of a reign of blood.
They found them both hacked to pieces
In a blood-darkened puddle of mud.

Jake Moody (10)
Acle St Edmund Primary School

BEETHOVEN

Beethoven is my dog,
He truly is the best,
But sometimes he's a hog,
And sometimes he's a pest.

He is a golden Labrador,
Very loving and playful,
He gets the post from the door,
And puts it on the table.

He sits and watches passers by,
(The horses in the summer,)
He really is a lovely dog,
I would not want another.

Daniel Rehders (11)
Acle St Edmund Primary School

VAMPIRES

Vampires, vampires,
They hate the light,
And wouldn't mind a fight.
They drink your blood,
Stab them with wood,
Into the heart,
Then they depart,
In their second fiery death.

They walk into your room,
No shadows, no souls,
No reflections in the water inside the bowls,
Walking strongly towards your bed,
Wanting to suck your blood till you're dead.

Vampires, vampires,
Oh, hear them snarl and creep,
They come when you're asleep,
People hear the snarls and think,
'Vampires? - No way!
I must be hearing things today!'

Joe Ridley (10)
Acle St Edmund Primary School

HORSES

I have three horses that I ride
Walk, trot, canter, always full of pride.
They eat juicy hay
All night and all day,
And in a stable is where they lay
With a bed of straw
On the stable floor.
When they're in a mood
Don't worry, just give them some food.
I go galloping in open fields
I go over jumps and tree stumps.
When you turn them out into their fields
They'll go for a stroll
And then for a roll
And eat lush grass
As bold as brass.

Emma Bowles (11)
Acle St Edmund Primary School

THE LITTLE SUNFLOWER SEEDS

There were some little
Sunflower seeds,
Who liked everything
Except weeds.

What they said was
'Weeds are *horrible*
Because they say
That we are edible!'

Beth James (9)
Acle St Edmund Primary School

PUSSY

Pussy caught some naughty little mice,
But I think Pussy is very nice.
I went fishing and Pussy came too,
Pussy caught a fish that was yellow and blue.
Pussy ruined my very best work,
So I called Pussy a silly old jerk.
I told Pussy to just go away,
Then Pussy sulked for the rest of the day.
I said, 'Pussy, I'm very sorry!'
Pussy didn't speak; I began to worry.
Next pussy miaowed in a hungry voice,
So I gave Pussy the food of his choice.
Whilst Pussy ate his meal, I had some peas,
But he started to itch - Pussy had fleas.
I ran to the vets, 'Oh, help me please!'
My beautiful cat has ugly fleas.
My Pussy is very special to me,
If you were his owner you would see.

Abigail Creak (10)
Acle St Edmund Primary School

MY SHADOW

I walk down the street at night,
Suddenly I have a fright.
Just as I walk past a light,
I see my shadow.

George Townend (9)
Acle St Edmund Primary School

SUMMER

Summer, summer, flowers sweet,
Butterfly flutter in midday heat.

Summer, summer, salty sea,
Buckets of fun for you and me.

Summer, summer, bright blue sky,
Clouds and birds go passing by.

Summer, summer, meadows green,
Daffodils and daisies are always seen.

Summer, summer, berries red,
Wet, dull weather now is dead.

Summer, summer, what a day,
I hope the summer will stay this way!

Jennifer Beck (11)
Acle St Edmund Primary School

MY SAILING POEM

I sail with a boat
I cross like a goat.
I speed along with the whistling wind
With a great big smile.
I wisp along the reeds
Rustle, rustle
With a great big smile.

Chris Frary (10)
Acle St Edmund Primary School

SHIPWRECK OF THE SHARKS

The shipwreck's silent,
Apart from the shifting of the sharks.
From the seabed you can see a cloudy something up ahead,
But what was that?
A movement that was sudden like a bomb.
Someone screamed like a lion roaring,
As I swam ahead something touched me.
Oh! Suddenly I was in pain from head to toe.
I swam, but I couldn't get there,
Now it was all a blur.
But what is that?
It's someone here beside me.
'Come on, let's go,' said a smooth and comfortable voice in my ear.

Rebekah Towler (9)
Acle St Edmund Primary School

THAT IS SO UNFAIR MUM

Time to go to school Kevin.
That is so unfair!
Make your bed Kevin.
I am not your slave!
Just do up your shoes Kevin.
You are so lazy!
If you want your breakfast, come and make it Kevin.
It's your problem! Mums these days can't do a thing
                                        for themselves!

Oscar Farnese (10)
Acle St Edmund Primary School

AUNTIE AGGIE

Aunt Aggie was cleaning,
What was the meaning?
Where did she go?
Nobody knows.
Just as my cup overflows,
But with no doubt,
It threw the old bag out.

I gave Dad a shout,
But he was fixing the watering can spout.
She came out with a boom,
So I got the broom
And shoved her right back up,
But then I sat on my cup.
I'll dust it up,
And buy a new cup.

Just for my Aunt Aggie,
Who is still stuck in the baggie,
I blew her up,
So I need another new cup,
Just for my Aunt Aggie.

Oh, I loved my aunt,
There just isn't a chance
For her to be living,
But hang on, what's that shivering?
Is that my Aunt Aggie?

It was, it was,
'Cause,
That's my strong Aunt Aggie.
Oh yes, my Aunt Aggie,
Who once got stuck up a baggie.
Oh, Aunt Aggie, Aunt Aggie, you go girl,
Do your special twirl,
Go, go, Aunt Aggie.

Steven Gowing (10)
Acle St Edmund Primary School

THE SNOW

Snowflakes falling
Gently from the sky
Laying on rooftops
And treetops up high.

Sweeping softly
Towards the ground
Covering everything
Without a sound.

Children come out
Wrapped up warm
To play in the wake
Of the snowstorm.

When the sun melts
The snow goes away
Maybe the snow
Will fall again some day . . .

Lily Smith (9)
Acle St Edmund Primary School

THE STORMY DAY

I sit before the window pane,
Looking out upon the rain.
Wet sheep grazing on the land,
Guided by the shepherd's hand.
Below, the stream swirls, swollen, running,
Through stinging bolts of lightning.
The oak struck down before my eyes;
Frightened, I hide from stormy skies.
On bended knees I shouted, 'Please,
Stop this storm at once and ease,
My fears and troubles whisk away,
Along with clouds and stormy day.'

Rachael Leech (10)
Acle St Edmund Primary School

SPINNY THE SPIDER

Spinny the spider
Is black and hairy
If you see him
You would find him scary.

Spinny's best friend is Dangly Deb
Who, at lunchtimes, likes to visit his web
Patiently they wait, watching with all their eyes
Just waiting, not too long
For their next batch of flies.

Yasmin Abassi (10)
Acle St Edmund Primary School

HORRIFYING HALLOWE'EN

Thunder, lightning
Hallowe'en!
Ghosts, ghouls
Scream!
Wizards, witches
Help!
Skeletons, bats
Yelp!
Full moon, werewolves
Screams filled
With horror!
Crazy castle here I
Leave!

Lauren Fulcher (10)
Acle St Edmund Primary School

ON MY OWN

On my own,
Pretending he's beside me,
My problems have all gone,
There's no one to deprive me,
But then I feel that he is standing by me,
But then I glance and he is just a river,
     I love him,
     I love him,
     I love him,
     On my own.

Henry Nicholls (9)
Acle St Edmund Primary School

THE LOCH NESS MONSTER

The Loch Ness monster,
Lives in Scotland,
Lives in a loch,
In the dark, murky depths.

Nobody ever sees it,
Nobody ever hears it,
But I know it's there.

There must be a reason,
For all the splashes,
All the moans,
All the groans -
There must be.

Laura Bilverstone (10)
Acle St Edmund Primary School

HELLO STRANGER

Hello stranger
I know you're out there somewhere
Your face glows when I see it
Your eyes sparkle like the stars
I know you're out there somewhere
I'm here
My friends are here
And you're here
Hello stranger.

Sophie Bedwell (8)
Acle St Edmund Primary School

I TRAVELLED AROUND THE WORLD

I travel around the world, day and night.
I need to find a place to stay,
And that gives me a very big fright.
I travel round the moon, don't give it away,
I can't fly my kite at night.
I go round planets too, please, don't give it away,
That does get me into a fright.
My best bit is day.
I don't like it at the end, because I have to go to bed at night,
Then my dreams start and my imagination takes flight.

Amy Haskett (9)
Acle St Edmund Primary School

ALL THE DIFFERENT SPORTS

Sports are probably my favourite thing!
As I'm not one to sit around doing nothing.

Netball is fun,
Especially when played out in the sun.

Swimming is the best,
But after an hour you need a rest.

Football is OK,
But I'd rather play croquet.

When I skip,
I always slip.

Georgia Hood (9)
Acle St Edmund Primary School

THE HUGE SANDWICH

'How do I make a sandwich?' asked Ben.
Mother said, 'Ask the hen.'
He got a huge piece of bread
And then he said . . .
'Get me some ham,
Get me a lamb,
Get me some cheese please.
Get Louise,
Get chips
And crisps
For tea for me.
Get ice cream,
Get normal whipped cream,
Don't forget beef.'
Oh no! Mum's come in.
What a mess!
'Where did you get all this?'
'From the supermarket.'
Put in some egg
And nutmeg
For we are having a feast.
Potatoes,
Tomatoes, we'll have the lot.
Milkshake,
Lots of cake.
Put in berries,
Don't forget the cherries.
Put in the last slice of bread.
Now where should I start?
I know, the ice cream.

Stephanie Hall (9)
Acle St Edmund Primary School

CATS

I've always loved cats,
But always hated bats.
Bats are so horrible,
And cats are so loveable.
I'm called Hollie,
And my cat is called Mollie.
She comes and sleeps on my bed,
Then goes downstairs and gets fed.
I have another cat called Millie,
She is very silly.
She drinks the water out of the big bath,
She looks so funny, she makes me laugh.
Peppy is the oldest cat,
She is so old she'd never catch a rat.
Peppy purrs all the time,
Though she is just so fine.
Ham is their best food,
When they're in a hungry mood.
They always purr,
When you stroke their fur.
They've got a wet, pink nose,
And cute, little toes.
Mollie and Millie run around the house,
Trying to catch a toy mouse.
Mollie nibbles my toes,
Then I can feel her wet, little nose.
Peppy has a basket for a bed,
Where she can rest her sleepy head.
Cats are the most affectionate pet,
Better than any other animal I've ever met!

Hollie Lynch (10)
Acle St Edmund Primary School

THE SUNSHINE

The sunshine is the world,
The sunshine is the sky,
The sunshine is when
We are having fun.
I say the sunshine is for us to see,
The sunshine is in the sky
Because it wants you to be -

Happy.

Chelsea Peacher (9)
Acle St Edmund Primary School

MY BOX

My box is at my grandma's.
Near my box is a spare bed.
Below my box is a little cabinet.
Above my box is a ceiling.
My box is made out of wood.
It is covered with flowers
And underneath the flowers
It is green like the grass.
It is not very heavy.
It has a lock on it.
My box is cuboid.
You have to open it with a key.
It doesn't make a sound.
In my box there are my special necklaces
With a cross on them.
I feel safe with them
Because Jesus is with the crosses.
When I close my box
I feel safe and happy.

Hannah Riches (10)
Carleton Rode VA Primary School

MY BOX

My box is in my bedroom
On a shelf underneath some flannels.
Near my box is my window
My box is below my wind chimes
And it is above my bed
My box is made from wood
The colour is bright pink with diamonds on
It is a really, really heavy box
It is shaped like a diamond
You just lift the top off to open it
Inside my box is my money
When I close my box
It makes a squeaky noise.

Leanne Frost (10)
Carleton Rode VA Primary School

MY HIDDEN TREASURES

My hidden treasures are my senses
With my eyes I see the beautiful gardens
With my ears I hear the birds singing
With my mouth I taste nice things,
Like chocolate and orange juice
With my nose I smell flowers from the gardens
I love my hidden treasures
And I will treasure them
For as long as I have them.

Alice Hambleton (11)
Carleton Rode VA Primary School

My Box

My box is in an empty house
Near my box is a creaky staircase
And an ancient radiator
Below my box is a scrap of carpet
Above my box is the ceiling
It is made of card
It is brown
It's covered in dust and Sellotape
It is a cube-shaped box
It has an embroidered lid made of string
I open my box by cutting the string
Spoiling the pattern
I look in my box
I see the toys
My best friend told me she had lost
I feel I should give back the toys
Because my friend lives far away
I shall look at the toys for a while
I hear my brother calling for me
I will put the box back
No wait, I am going to see my friend today
Should I give them back?
I am not sure
What do you think?

Chloe Payne (9)
Carleton Rode VA Primary School

MY BOX

My box is in my loft,
Near my box is a chest of dusty drawers,
Below my box is the wooden floor,
Above my box is the tall roof,
My box is resting on another big box,
My box is made of pinewood,
My box is a light sandy colour,
My box has got a flower on the front,
My box has got no hinges,
My box is a rectangle,
My box has got a padlock
Then it opens and there's a number code
Then a plastic cover,
It can only be opened by my hands,
Inside my box is a ring because it's magic,
The box opens and power of light comes out,
The colour is red and has got metal on it,
When I open the box I feel magical,
I'm going to do magic with it
And hide it away from everybody but me,
When I close my box
It shoots out green power to close it,
Then it closes on its own,
I put it away
And I hide the key from everybody else.

Katie Boak (11)
Carleton Rode VA Primary School

MY BOX

My box is in a dusty cellar,
Near my box there is a letter.
Below my box there is a cold, dusty floor,
Above my box there is a smashed light.

My box is made of beautiful dark wood,
On the side of my box there is a carved code.
My box has shiny, gold hinges,
My box is small and light.
It is in the shape of a curvy heart.

My box has a steel padlock,
Attached to it is a rusty, iron key.
I open my box,
It is only light, but it is still very stiff.
As I am still carefully opening it,
I hear it creaking.

Click! My box is open,
Inside my box there is a gold necklace.
I get the necklace
And carefully slip it around my neck.
I close my box,
It shuts with a silent click.

Bryony Slatter (11)
Carleton Rode VA Primary School

SPECIAL PLACE

There is a place where the sun shines all day
And at sunset
It glows a dozen shades
Of orange, yellow and red
Waves on the beach
Lap over the shining sand
And a quiet, gentle tide
Moves slowly along
Palm trees' leaves dip in the water
People on boats
Trailing their fingers
There are many different animals
Like deer and doe
With smooth, silky skin
And soft, innocent eyes
I want to be
In my special place
Forever.

Hafsa Zayyan (11)
Colman Middle School

THE HEAVEN FLOWER

The Heaven flower, standing proud,
As gold as Heaven,
In the middle of the forest.
Sticky like sap, thorny like a rose,
Rarer than the rest,
The most beautiful flower in the world,
Few remain, because of man's shame.

Ross Buxton (10)
Colman Middle School

MY FAMILY

My family always plays football with me
They help me with my homework
They pay money for trips that I can go on
They let me sleep over at friends
They sometimes take me out somewhere
They let me go to the park with my sisters
They sometimes let me have a McDonald's
They kiss me goodnight
They say goodbye when I go to school
They always come to the hospital if I hurt myself
They let me stay up late
They buy gifts when they are in the city
I can always trust them.

Jenna Tye (10)
Colman Middle School

CYBERWORLD

Cyberworld is the i-max cinema
Put on your 3D glasses
All-round sound effects
Making it so real.
Fantasy worlds like another planet
Underwater creatures swim by
As if they come into the cinema
Feeling as if you are actually there
A screen covering the whole wall
Stunning effects.

George Bell (11)
Colman Middle School

FRIENDS

Friends are like your mum
They like helping you when you're stuck
Give you Christmas and birthday cards
Are kind and helpful
Friends will tell you jokes to cheer you up
Encourage you when you're doing something right
Always playing games with you
Sleeping round yours
They share their stuff
And like the things you like
They walk to school with you
I'd be lost without my friends.

Lauren Hutton (10)
Colman Middle School

SOMEONE SPECIAL

I know someone special
Who is very kind to me
Someone I like very much
She cheers me up when I am sad and lonely
If I am stuck, she comes along to help me
This special person shares her things with me
We care for each other like we are family
She is my best friend
I can trust her
She can trust me
That person knows me so well
It's nice to see a cheerful face
That's why I like her so much.

Georgia Havers (11)
Colman Middle School

HARRY GEORGE POTTER

Harry is my brother,
He is very special,
He has soft, silky hair,
A softly, lightly, baby-touched skin,
He is my best and only brother,
Cheeky, bright smile,
Always glad to see me,
Likes having food fights with me,
Slumbers silently, peacefully in his sleep,
He's got a special baby smell,
Like he has been sprayed with perfume,
A very cute laugh,
Always very chatty,
Made in a special way, just for me!

Rosy Potter (10)
Colman Middle School

MY TEDDY

He's warm and cuddly next to me in bed.
His furry ears are always listening to people talking together.
His black, beady eyes watching for danger.
His dark velvet nose sniffs delicious smells.
His colourful bow tie brightens up his face.
His squashy tummy's like marshmallows.
His short, stubby tail is like candyfloss.
He's as small as a kitten.
He's brown like toffee and fudge.
He's as fuzzy as cotton wool.
That's what I like about him.

Stevie Riddell (11)
Colman Middle School

MY BED

My bed carries me into a dream-like slumber.
I'm in a horse-pulled chariot on my way to Dream City.
When I arrive at Dream City I trot off the golden chariot.
There are ecstatic people in the same dream as mine.
Dream city is colourific.
There are stars like wonders and a sun like a light which
makes me feel warm.
I am happier than the happiest person in the world.
As I sway in the light breeze,
I drift deeper into my dream.
I start to wake up, but when I open my eyes I see a man
and he owns life.
I then see my mum opening my curtains.
The sunlight brightens my day as it reminds me of the dream
I had.

Christopher Seaman (11)
Colman Middle School

KATIE

My dog Katie is two years old,
Playful, kind and loving,
Brown, white and spotty.
She sleeps under the quilt,
Yaps and barks,
Rolls in the mud,
Has a cold, wet nose.
She's a small Jack Russell,
She loves bones,
She's cute with wiry fur.

Jessica Thacker (11)
Colman Middle School

STARS

Shining like the moon,
Sparkling like a sparkler,
Glistening like fresh dew in the morning grass,
Glowing like the midday sun,
Beautiful and glamorous like a diamond,
Bright, beautiful and magical,
Dazzling in the darkness of the night sky,
Twinkling through the telescope,
Pretty and picturesque,
Magnificently magical,
Glinting like glitter,
Exquisite and energetic.

Kyle Brooks (11)
Colman Middle School

MY MUM

She is sweet,
She helps me with my homework.
Sometimes she will buy me things,
She will let me go to the park,
She will let my friends stay over.
Sometimes she will let me decorate my room.
If she has time she will take me to the cinema,
After she will take me to McDonald's.
My mum is very special.

Lisa-Jane Kerton (10)
Colman Middle School

DIAMONDS

Shining like silver spoons,
Bright and sparkly,
Rare and shimmering against any star,
A priceless, beautiful piece of brilliance.
Colours bright,
A magnificent competitor for any star.
Sparkling like brand new alloy wheels,
Slippery and wet looking.
Flashing like Christmas lights.
Magical colours,
Vibrantly beautiful against most models.

Billy Fisher (11)
Colman Middle School

THE RIVER BANK

Rivers gently flowing by
Fish leaping up to the rain
Ducks paddling down the stream
And swans showing their spectacular wing span
Flowers shining with droplets on the bank
Grass waving at the breeze
Stones rolling underwater
Leaves drifting onto the water
Then going down with the current
Dogs running to sniff the plants
And seagulls screeching over treetops.

Joshua Wheeler (10)
Colman Middle School

Snow

Snowflakes fall softly from the sky like cotton wool.
To be able to watch snow has a beautiful feeling
Like seeing the stars in the night sky.
The snowflakes fall gracefully onto the ground,
Like a ballerina finishing a leap.
It looks like a blanket on a bed of earth.
The snow glistens on the ground like diamonds and rubies.
Animals hibernate from the snow and cold
Like snails in their shell.
The snow is deep and like a gigantic flat freezer, but fun.
Snow has its own special colour, its own magical white
Like a rainbow has its own individual reds, yellows and greens.
When it melts, it's all slushy, it's not snow anymore.
People trudge in the snow and turn it grey, like mould.
Then it's gone, like air, and can't come back.

Valeska Hall (10)
Colman Middle School

Childhood

I learnt my ABC and I was ready for my 1, 2, 3.
When I was ready for my own room, I could sleep in it alone.
The first time I fell and hurt myself, tears came from me.
I first started to walk and I said my first words.
Once I stepped inside my school, I was scared and frightened too.
I had tied my hair in two bunches, they were jumping pigtails.

Nazmin Ali (11)
Colman Middle School

SWEETS 'R' US

Scrumdidillyumptious sweets rumble in your tum.
Fluffy, squelchy, bouncy marshmallows.
Toffee hard or soft anything will do.
Dib-Dab, Dib-Dab with the sherbet lolly.
Liquorice tips, a strawberry delight.
A Crunchie like a beehive with a honeycomb centre.
Stomp, stomp, stomp with the Chomp.
Sherbet cocktail like a frying pan on your tongue.
Extra, extra, extra hard, hard gums.
A Toblerone standing like a pyramid.
Jelly beans that rock like a rocking horse.
Mars, far, far away.

Thomas Mills (10)
Colman Middle School

FLUFFY

Licking me better when I'm upset.
Purring loudly, feeling happy.
Eating food and making a mess.
Being good and getting treats.
Playing cat games with his friends.
Fur like black and white velvet.
Soft and silky like ribbon.
Standing proud in his collar.

Gemma Mundy (11)
Colman Middle School

COMPUTERS

I sit down on my chair
Switch on the computer
Put in game 'Age of Empires II'
Click on 'start game'
People and islands for my war
Click on 'begin game'
Type in cheats for people
We fight
Then the enemy resigns
I am victorious
Then 'start new game'.

Christopher Ward (10)
Colman Middle School

PLAYFUL

My cat is called Playful.
He cheers me up when I am sad.
He is soft, cute and cuddly.
He makes me laugh.
His ears are as pointy as foxes.
He prowls like a tiger under the moonlight.
His eyes sparkle like sapphires.
Playful is active and energetic.
I love him how he is.

Leanne Black (10)
Colman Middle School

LOST AT SCHOOL

I found myself lost,
I'm not quite sure where.
I spotted my reflection
And all I do is stare.

My hair is a mess,
My clothes all a tatter.
I'm really untidy,
But that doesn't matter.

It's non-uniform day
And I don't know what to wear,
Everything's all worn and scruffy,
But I don't really care.

Charlotte Newell (10)
Falcon Middle School

LOST FOR WORDS

I'm lost for words,
And what to say,
Got to write a poem,
And I'll be here all day.

I'm lost for words,
It's gone all wrong,
Rhymes jump off the paper,
My verses are too long.

I'm lost for words,
They disappear,
There's nothing in my head
. . . err . . . what next?

Jennifer Hardman (10)
Falcon Middle School

LOST ON MARS

I can't believe I've been to space.
It's such a beautiful, starry place.
When I landed on solid air
I hadn't imagined it so bare.
The planet I was on must've been Mars,
I could tell because of the shooting stars.
Over rocks and hills I race,
My legs wobble and my shoes unlace.
Sweat is dripping down my head,
I wish I was on Earth, lying on my bed.
I saw a spaceship speeding by
An alien came out and said, 'Hi!'
He asked me if I wanted a lift
And before I knew it I was home in a shift.

Laura Fearnley (9)
Falcon Middle School

LOST IN A BOOK

Before I was lost I was reading a book,
Then I looked around a strange place.
Not like at home.
It didn't feel right.
Then when was that?
I froze in terror.
It settled on my face.
Writing?
It must have been a dream.
One day I'd like to visit that place again.
Wait a minute, where am I?

Tom Cullum (9)
Falcon Middle School

THE LOST RUNAWAY

A smoky path on the track,
Fumes of steam fill the air,
Upon this rusty road,
The wheels a clatter above the bars,
And wavy flames smoulder the coal,
Upon this rusty road,
That old train, steaming train,
Red and yellow coloured train,
Upon this rusty road,
It's lost around the steel rods,
Never will it end,
Upon this rusty road,
But then the train, it sees a light!
On the darkened night,
Upon this rusty road,
It bounces closer, and closer to the light,
The flashing brightened light,
Upon this rusty road,
Green hills, the train goes on,
Trundling day and night,
Upon this rusty road,
Then the track ends right near the light,
But the light is high above,
Upon this rusty road,
A giant tower of bricks the light had settled,
Racing high above, in the sky,
Upon this rusty road,
The train looked up to see,
And wondered what it was,
A lighthouse, now it's home and its life will still live on.

Daniel Lawrence (10)
Falcon Middle School

LOST IN A MATHS LESSON

I'm lost in a maths lesson,
There are numbers everywhere,
1, 2, 3 and 4,
They're spinning in my head,
They're whirling, twirling, going round.
Suddenly, here comes a maths sheet and on it says,
'72 x 56' and I don't have a clue,
The teacher comes forward and looks me in the eye,
I stutter and I stammer and then I say,
'Is it um . . . er . . . 362?'
'Correct,' he says, 'good girl, well done!'
I'm lost in a maths lesson,
There are numbers everywhere,
1, 2, 3 and 4,
They're spinning in my head.

Ellie Rogers (10)
Falcon Middle School

LOST IN LONDON

My eyes are weeping,
Vision is blurred,
Crowds rushing around.

Stomach rumbling,
I slowly walk on,
Big Ben has struck,
Must be lunchtime.

I feel my pockets
For forgotten change.
What's that big lump?
It's a sweet wrapper.

Can't be much use,
Wish I could go home,
That's where I am,
Back at home in bed.

Charlotte Clarke (10)
Falcon Middle School

LOST IN A DREAM

Across the seas and over grasslands
Is a wild jungle of dreams.
Talking monkeys and chirping children
Is all I seem to see.
Suddenly a dragon leaps to his feet
And with scorching violent breath
He hurls me into a deep, dark forest
Where I'm sure to meet my death.
I hear a rustle, a tall dark figure appears.
All at once my eyes start to sting,
My vision blurs and my heart beats rapidly.
But I can smell the sweet scent of perfume,
I can see clearly now.
Wait a minute, I recognise that face,
Reality returns.

Katherine Green (10)
Falcon Middle School

LOST IN A MUMMY'S TOMB

I stumble.
It's dark, cold and wet,
I only went in for a bet.
Now I'm scared and want to go home,
It's frightening being all alone.

I stumble.
Rats dashing across my feet,
Looking for scraps of food to eat.
Ancient writing covers the wall,
What's that sound, did someone call.

I stumble.
Spiders' cobwebs in my face,
My heart beats faster, then starts to race.
I see the tomb, shiny gold,
I shouldn't be here, I've been told.

I stumble.
I have to touch it, that was the deal,
Does the mummy know how scared I feel?
I touch it, my task is done,
Not it's time to turn and run.

I stumble.
From behind the rocks I see the light,
I push and shove with all my might.
They fall away, I'm out, I'm out,
I jump with joy, I scream and shout.

Thomas Coe (10)
Falcon Middle School

LOST IN A MAGICAL LAND

I was lost in a magical land,
Where there were shops selling magic wands,
There are witches flying overhead,
And kids asking their mums for sweets
I thought to myself, how will I get out?
I walked into a very old shop,
There was an old man standing behind the counter.
He looked at me curiously,
And started fiddling with his wand.
I walked out again, straight away.
For on sale were
Some glass eyes and a hand,
And other horrible stuff.
I walked down the street,
There was a shop called 'Kids Only'
I walked in,
This time the walls were red, yellow and blue.
There were some teenagers standing under a sign saying,
'How to make a part of your body vanish and reappear'
And underneath it were some extra fingers.
And I thought to myself,
I wish I could get home
And, *bang!*
I started spinning and spinning,
I looked around.
There were all the colours of the rainbow spinning around me
I started to get panicky, when would it end?

Simon Watts (9)
Falcon Middle School

LOST IN A MAZE

I'm lost in a maze and I don't know where to go.
Do I turn left? Do I turn right?
Do I turn here? Do I turn there?
I've lost my mum!
I hunt frantically everywhere.
I feel like my tummy's turning inside out.
What do I do? Where do I go?
I run around and round the place,
Like a huge gorilla on the loose.
I finally manage to find my mum,
She's looking for me too.
I run to her, she runs to me.
I hug her very tight.
I'm not lost anymore, I'm found.

Hayley Braithwaite (9)
Falcon Middle School

LOST IN TIME

Twirling, whirling,
Fuzzing, buzzing.
Around I go,
Spinning through time.
Dinosaurs and monsters,
Fairytale creatures.
I'm getting dizzy,
There are the Romans,
There are the Celts.
I'm in the future,
I'm in the past.
I'm on my bed,
Home at last.

Natalie Edwards (9)
Falcon Middle School

LOST UNDERGROUND

I am lost under the ground,
I don't know where I'm going,
I don't know where I'll be found.

I've been digging for a day,
I don't know where to go,
I don't know which way.

I am getting very worried,
My brain is starting to get hurried,
My head is spinning round and round,
What if I'm never found?

Wait a minute, I've been here before,
There's my pillow and there's the door!
I'm not in a tunnel,
I was wrong!
I've been under the covers all along!

William Wynne (10)
Falcon Middle School

LOST IN A SPELLING TEST

I'm lost in a spelling test,
There's letters everywhere.
ABCD,
I don't know which letter to choose.
I'm sweating and I'm worried,
ABC and D?
Will the teacher pick on me?

Sophie Carpenter (9)
Falcon Middle School

LOST

Help!
I'm lost in the woods,
It's dark,
I'm scared.
What was that?
A wolf? A lion?
I don't care,
I'm getting out of here.
Now where am I?
A deep swamp.
It's scary and smelly.
What's that?
A car?
A truck?
No, it's a helicopter
Come to rescue me.

Jack Betts (10)
Falcon Middle School

LOST IN A SPELLING TEST

I'm lost in a spelling test,
Which letter should I choose?
The time is ticking on,
I'm probably going to lose,
It's a very hard decision,
It's very hard to choose,
Now the minute is over,
ABC or lose?

Yelena Buck (10)
Falcon Middle School

LOST IN SPACE

I'm lost in space,
Whose is that face?
Is it on the moon?
I hope I'm home soon.

Rockets fly by,
High in the sky,
I wish I could fly,
So high in the sky.

There's a black hole,
Without a mole,
Millions of stars
And look, there is Mars.

Luke Anderson (10)
Falcon Middle School

LOST TIME

Clock is slowing,
Drowning voices,
Vision blurring,
I can't find my way.

Concentration falling,
My mind is spinning,
Lights are flickering,
My mind has gone.

Whirling, swirling,
Swishing, twirling,
Spinning . . . gone,
Lost time.

Hannah Moss (10)
Falcon Middle School

EVENING AND MORNING

Yellow star,
Oh so bright,
You shine through my window,
And light up the night.

Oh bright moon,
I watch as I lay,
Your flickering beams,
Chase the shadows away.

As I lay dreaming,
Of a life full of fun,
I wake and I find
The bright golden sun.

Day has arrived,
The dark's gone away,
I jump out of my bed,
To start a new day.

Another adventure,
New thoughts in my head,
A day full of fun,
Then it's time for my bed.

Bonita Davies (9)
Falcon Middle School

GETTING LOST IN THE ATLANTIC

If you ever get lost in the Atlantic
You'll feel extremely petrified.
But take my advice
I am quite nice,
When you hear a lobster groan,
Dive deep down to the flame-red coral seam,
Touch the Titanic's battered ruins
This is not so difficult, is it?
It will bounce you up like a trampoline,
Heave yourself onto the sandbank
Then find your mum and dad.
They won't say you are bad
Just because you found a secret pearl.

Daniel Cotton (9)
Falcon Middle School

THE SEASIDE

The seaside is one of the best of places,
To see the smiles on people's faces.
I don't even mind the seaside pong,
When I hear that mermaid song.
I'd love to look at the shells all day,
But unfortunately forever I can't stay.
Hopefully you will go to the beach one day,
And maybe you'll see the mermaids play.

Rosa Whitman (10)
Gresham Village School

DETENTION ALL WEEK

Over the moon,
three times around Mars,
we landed on Pluto to stay for a week,
eight hours later I had a little peek
at some aliens
and as soon as I stopped looking
and what could I see
I was surrounded by little round spaceships.
One of the aliens said, 'Shall we hit him with a rock?'
Then I awoke to a loud roaring noise,
to a monster with hundreds of eyes.
I jumped to my feet and I blinked my eyes
I was asleep, it was just a dream
then the next thing I saw
was my teacher with a frowning face,
she stuck a bit of paper in front of my eyes
and in large red writing it said,
'detention all week'!

Harriet Woodman (8)
Gresham Village School

LAUGHTER

Laughter only comes out
when there is something funny about,
and when he's finished laughing
he goes back to his deep, dark place
somewhere in your heart.
If you by any chance meet Laughter,
he will dive out of the way,
quick as a flash, back to his hiding place.

Tom Maingay (10)
Gresham Village School

I BELIEVE IN . . .

I believe in aliens and Martians
From outer space.
With their goggly eyes and ugly faces
They can't even tie their lace.
They live far away
Maybe one day they'll come and play.

I believe in fairies and elves,
Who help clean up your bedroom and shelves,
And when you lose a tooth,
From under your pillows they'll take it
And swap it for a pound,
Without making any sound.

I believe in monsters
Those ugly scary beasts
That live under your bed.
You always wonder if they've been fed,
Will they eat you up at night
Or just give you a nasty fright?
They might have a nibble at your toes,
So beware of having a dose!

Kerry Kinsley (10)
Gresham Village School

AUTUMN

A bove the leafy carpet,
U nder the stormy sky,
T rees standing naked,
U tterings of cold weather,
M entions of snow,
N othing beats an autumn day.

Claire Wilton (10)
Gresham Village School

MYSELF

C is for creativity, a world of vibrant patterns.
H umourous and funny, her personality is a cure for depression.
R ich in talent, the star of every show.
I   magination is her best friend.
S ecretive and special, her sparkling eyes tell it all.
T he Valentine's girl I am!
O h, what a marvellous birthday!
B is for beauty, her pre-Raphaelite curls.
E is for extraordinary elegance, a gift that comes naturally.
L is for living. That's what she loves to do!

Christobel Hastings-Knowles (9)
Gresham Village School

MY MUM

My mum is beautiful,
She is most definitely
The most pretty woman in the world.
I love my mum,
She is very funny
And she cares for me.
She is 100% the best mum
Anyone could wish for.
We think she's a genie
Because whatever we could wish for
She has inside her.

Peter Wilton (9)
Gresham Village School

NO SUCH THING AS MAGIC

My mum and dad say, 'There's no such thing as magic',
But then there was the story at school which was very tragic.
It happened like this;
In class 7 something went wrong
When they were learning about Hong Kong.
A boy called Martin burst.
His guts spilled out
And everyone started to shout.
The teacher went ballistic,
Then a wizard appeared,
With a striped, ruffled beard,
And with a zap of his candle
Martin was put together
(Though some of his body parts were in the wrong place!)

Lily Walker (8)
Gresham Village School

FOOD

Strawberries with chocolate sauce and cream.
Jacket potatoes with cheese in the seam.
Chicken soups and spaghetti hoops,
That's what I like best.

Carrots and peas
Honey made by bees.
Chinese curries and McDonald's McFlurries,
That's what I *detest*!

Sophie Cowper Johnson (11)
Gresham Village School

THE BUMBLEBEE

Once Bobby Bumblebee fell in some honey,
and his family found it quite funny.
He jumped out in one big leap,
and fell in one massive heap.
'Ouch!' he cried in a mumble and grumble
as he landed on a biscuit crumble.
'You're injured, go straight to bed,' Mum said,
'Cuddle and snuggle up tight with Ted.'

Dawn Mallett (11)
Gresham Village School

THE RABBIT CALLED BEAUTY

There was a rabbit called Beauty
Who had a lovely owner
She fed him and gave him water
She cared for him and she loved him
And every winter she brought him indoors
So she could feed him and water him and he wouldn't get cold.

Beauty is brown and white
In summer she holds him tight
She plays lots of games with him
Like 'It' and 'Follow the Leader'
And he really enjoys it in the summer.
In autumn she puts all the leaves in a pile and Beauty jumps in them.
One day she says,
I don't want him anymore.
Beauty is very upset
And in a few hours
Because he is so sad
He dies and then she regrets what she said.

Victoria Crisp (11)
Heartsease Middle School

ANIMALS IN THE WILD

Animals neigh,
Animals moo,
Just look at the cow
And the horse too.

The wild has all of the animals there,
With noises too,
The bodies are different
Which is sometimes like you.

Animals go fast,
Animals go slow,
Just like the cheetah
And the snail too.

Animals bite,
Animals snore,
Just like the owl
And the shark too.

Animals glide,
Animals leap,
Just like the seagull,
And the frog too.

They're not like us,
Just so you know,
So go and see them,
Run and jump
And think what you know,
So go, go, go, go.

Jack Ives-Keeler (8)
Heartsease Middle School

MY FAMILY

'Can you play?'
'Hurry up.'
'Get out.'
That's my brother.

'Eat up.'
'Be good.'
'Don't slam the door.'
That's my mum.

'Wait a minute.'
'What's that thing upstairs?'
'Don't shout.'
That's my dad.

'Be nice.'
'Sit down.'
'Shut the door.'
That's my nanny.

'Go to bed.'
'No, it's dinner in a minute.'
'Sit down and eat up.'
That's my grandad.

It isn't even quiet at night
Because of my dog going 'Woof, woof!'

Ethan Holloway (9)
Heartsease Middle School

DON'T DO THIS, DO THAT

Don't do this!
Don't do that!
Don't do this!

That's my mum going on!

Get me this!
Get me that!
Get me this!

That's my dad going on!

Go to school!
Go to play!
Go to lunch!

That's my teacher going on!

Ebony Dawson (9)
Heartsease Middle School

JOLLY OLD SANTA

Santa is jolly, Santa is fat,
Santa wears a red coat and hat.
He climbs down chimneys,
Puts presents around the tree,
He slips away quietly
While you're sleeping peacefully.
The presents are all nice and neat,
The cupboards are full
Of good things to eat,
So let's fill our bellies
With ice cream and jellies,
Oh boy, are we in for a treat!

Sally Hartle (9)
Heartsease Middle School

My Favourite Day

Christmas, Christmas
It's a special day,
It's the time
That Jesus was born in the hay.

Listening for Santa
Staying awake,
Can't wait until morning
And for the Christmas cake.

Presents are opened,
Dinner is made,
Relatives visit,
The table is laid.

The drinks are all flowing,
We're watching TV,
Playing with our presents,
How joyful are we.

The day is now ending,
It's time for our beds,
We're shutting our eyes
And laying down our heads.

Sharna Wright (10)
Heartsease Middle School

Wild Animals

Wild animals are wild
They run so fast and eat quickly.
Tigers and lions are my favourite animals.
I wish I could be with them all the time.

Dolphins and seals swim
Under the water so beautifully.
I wish I could swim under the water with them.
I dream things but they never come true.

Sarah Wilson (8)
Heartsease Middle School

MY TEACHER

My teacher is scary
With big black eyes.
She's horrible and hairy
And is full of lies.
She screams and shouts
She scratches her cheek
She argues with no doubts
And her nose is a beak.
Her nose holes are big
She smells of stew
In the garden she'll dig
And indoors she'll moo.
She eats off her lap
She slaps my friend Lee
She drinks from a tap
And she watches me wee.
She acts like a dog
She itches with fleas
She would fetch a log
And she would chase some bees
And that's my teacher Mrs Danger!

Michael Britt (10)
Heartsease Middle School

THE GRINCH

There was a thing called The Grinch
He did not move an inch
Max was his dog
And he ate like a hog.
They both did smell
And they looked like Hell
The Grinch is very mad
Because he is sad
He is very hairy
He's played by Jim Carrey.
He loves Martha May
He thinks of her all day
Martha may fell in love with The Grinch
He did not believe her so she gave him a pinch
They fell in love it's forever
They never left each other, no never.

Rebecca Jeary (10)
Heartsease Middle School

SPIDERS

Black and little and cute,
Hairy, brown or red,
Moving fast, moving slow,
Spinning webs,
Catching flies,
Friendly or poisonous,
I like little spiders.

Leanne Hannant (9)
Heartsease Middle School

UNDER THE FLOWER BED

Under the flower bed
There are worms and snails and ants
The worms slither across the soil
The snails slime across the soil
The ants jump on each other on the soil
They bury each other under the ground.

Jasmine Brown (9)
Heartsease Middle School

SILLY BILLY

There was a young man called Billy
he always looked very silly
he went into the shops
and came out with spots
and saw his girlfriend Tilly.

Perrie Greaves (10)
Heartsease Middle School

THE MAN IN THE SHED

There was a young man named Ted
Who lived in a box in a shed
One day he fell out
And smacked his snout
Then spent a long time in bed.

Natasha Burns (10)
Heartsease Middle School

DRAGON

Down in the woods there's a cave
And in that cave there's a
Horrible, snarling, fire-breathing *dragon!*

And in that *dragon*
There's glistening diamonds
And lovely golden gold!

The *dragon's* eyes
Are like bullets, always accurate
And his tail whooshes like lightning
And deep red body like blood
And teeth like daggers and that's the
Dragon!

Martin Westgate (9)
Heartsease Middle School

SNAKE

The snake slithers slowly along the ground,
It makes a funny hissing sound,
The snake hunts for prey at night,
It eats its prey in one big bite.
It does not give up food without a fight,
It will kill you in one big bite
And gives you a mighty fright.
Its venom is poisonous,
He really hates noises,
It lives underground,
It's where they don't get found,
It's really dark underground.

Max Banfield (9)
Heartsease Middle School

MY HOUSE

My hamster squeaks
He rolls in a ball
And he crashes into the chair
Not into the wall.

My hamster was called Harry Potter
He was brown and white
He was very cute
When he didn't bite.

He usually makes a funny noise
And he jumps on his house
He eats his food very quickly
And stuffs it in his mouth
And he makes a lot of mess
If you know what I mean
But I love him.

Joshua Hoy (8)
Heartsease Middle School

THE HAMSTER

The hamster always hides at night,
And then you never see him in sight,
He never comes out
Because he always hears me shout!
He sits in his plastic house
And then he makes noises like a mouse
He doesn't like cheese,
But he might like Chinese.
He's nice and curly
And he looks like a girly.

Lauren Bridge (9)
Heartsease Middle School

SPORT

I like to play football
I like to kick the ball
I like to pass and tackle
Then we go and score a goal!

I like to play tennis
I like to hit the ball
It's the last game in the final
Then I smash the ball and I win!

I like to play rugby
I like to pass
It's a draw in the last minute
Then we get a run
Hooray to the Bulls we have won!

I like to play basketball
I like to throw the ball
In the basketball net
Then I go and score because I am tall!

I like to play cricket
You hit the ball really far
They run and run for the ball
It's out of the pitch
We win the game
Two hundred and four runs to England!

Sam Durrant (9)
Heartsease Middle School

WINTER COMES, WINTER GOES

Winter comes, winter goes
With the cold wind blowing up your nose.
Little children having a snowball fight
Mums and dads sighing at the sight.
People wrapped up warm
In the blasting storm.
There are layers and layers of snow
Look I've sink, oh no.
Winter's gone, spring's here
Next summer's going to be near.
Then autumn flying by it goes,
Freezing stiff, old toes.
Back comes snowy winter
Oh look, I've got a nasty splinter.
Snowball fighting has just now started
The aeroplane in the air has just departed.
This is how the seasons go
Look I'm sinking in the snow, slow.
Over and over go the seasons,
There are lots of reasons
Why we should enjoy them all.
The dogs just ran into the wall
Now the seasons are all done
It's time to start having fun.

Roxanne Kelf (10)
Heartsease Middle School

THE BOYS AND GIRLS PHANTOM

Once upon a time the girls thought they were the best,
But the boys thought they were better than the rest.
Some of the boys heard the girls asking for a race,
But the leader of the gang didn't hear because he was tying his lace.
The leader of the gang said, 'What are you talking about?'
He said, 'But don't make me shout.'
They had a race, they ran with a fast pace,
They all had fun, because the boys won.

Emma Stone (10)
Heartsease Middle School

THE HORRID TEACHER

There once was a horrid, old teacher
Who swung people round by their hair
She used to pull real nice faces
But now she gives people a scare
She has really sparkly blue eyes
And hair which comes down to her feet
And when she goes out shopping
She hates everyone that she meets
She stares at us real evil
And hits us hard with the cane
And people think that where she lives
Is on a horrible, spooky lane
She doesn't have any children
Because she would treat them really bad
And if they were naughty
She would certainly go mad.

Emma Joy (10)
Heartsease Middle School

APPLE PIE, YUM! YUM!

A pple pie in my tum,
P lease make me more Mum,
P eople say,
L et's play,
E ven though we go,

P ie is scrummy,
I n my tummy,
E very one pie is . . .

Y um, yum!
U nder my chin.
M y mouth is waterin'!

Y um, yum!
U p we go, I rush home as it's
M onday and *apple pie day!*

Stevie Louise Childs (10)
Heartsease Middle School

THE SOUP SONG

All people like kinds of soup,
Some taste like tomato and some look like gloop.

They come in packs and in tins.

Some people like soup with sharks' fins,
And some people don't like soup.

Dayna Bobby (10)
Heartsease Middle School

THE SPOOKY HOUSE

Once upon a time I was walking in the woods
There was a big hill and it had a spooky house.
I walked up to the hill,
And I saw a windmill.
There were lots of spiders,
There were some tigers,
There was blood everywhere,
There was also underwear.
Then I saw a ghost, it was scary,
Then I saw a man, he was hairy.
I ran away, I couldn't escape,
I wrapped them up in Sellotape.

Olivia Lince-Andrade (10)
Heartsease Middle School

SCHOOL

Schooldays are the best days,
You learn, make friends, do plays.

Some teachers are good, some are bad,
You'll know which is which if you're a bad lad.

If I get too many detentions
It might lead to suspension.

But I like my school teachers and friends
And this is where my poem ends.

Sean Hankins (11)
Heartsease Middle School

Harry Potter Acrostic Poem

H   ermione Grainger
A   lbus Dumbledore
R   on Weasley
R   ubeus Hagrid
Y   oung wizard

P   hilosopher's Stone
O   llivanders
T   ransfiguration
T   he Lord Voldermort
E   nchantment
R   avenclaw, Hufflepuff, Slytherin, Gryffindor.

Arran Starling (10)
Heartsease Middle School

Dance Classes

One move or another,
It's like fighting with your brother.
Up, down, down then up,
Like you're trying for the cup.
Day, night, night and day,
I've forgotten the moves anyway.
Twists and turn, round you go,
With tapping shoes on your toes.
Right, left and left then right
I have a lesson tonight!

Sophie Young (11) & Heloise Bush (10)
Heartsease Middle School

CINDERELLA

Cinderella lived with her stepmother and two stepsisters,
Cinderella had to do all the mucky things in the house.
The stepmother got a letter,
A great invitation from the king to the grand ball,
The stepmother was jumping for joy,
The two stepsisters were hugging and kissing,
But poor old Cinderella was feeling sad and alone,
Cinderella was not going to the great ball.

The stepmother and stepsisters had danced to the ball,
Cinderella was very unhappy,
She stumbled outside and started to cry,
Cinderella's head arose, she saw her fairy godmother,
Cinderella jumped out of her skin,
Cinderella was shocked,
The fairy godmother made a horse and carriage,
She announced, 'Be back before 12 midnight!'

Natalie Curran (9)
Heartsease Middle School

THE RUGRATS

T   ommy is the boss of the bunch
H   e is super cool,
E   veryone loves him.

R   ugRats are simply the best,
U   nderneath their nappies lay
G   reen bugs and icky things,
R   ugRats beat all the rest.
A   ngelica is nasty,
T   easing all the babies
S   o what do you think?

Samantha Jones (10)
Heartsease Middle School

LUCKY THE RABBIT

There was a rabbit called Lucky
Who's cage was really mucky.

He likes to play around
And tries not to touch the ground.

His favourite food is bread,
But he doesn't like lead.

He loves to run
His treat is a bun.

His cage looks like a nest
When I clean it out, it will look the best.

Nathan Sadd (11)
Heartsease Middle School

THE FOOTIE MATCH

The score was two all
The ref started to call.

Norwich wore green
And the other team was mean.

There was a chant going round the ground
And the players kept going round and round.

Mark Rivers is the best
Robert Green saves the rest.

Melissa Moore (11)
Heartsease Middle School

THE GIRL WHO CRIED . . .

'Mum, I feel really ill
I'll stay at home and be good, I will
I'll be in bed all day
I promise I won't go out to play'
'Okay, just this one time,' Mum said
'If you promise to stay in bed.'

As soon as Mum went out the door
I got some chocolate and ate more and more
I fell asleep on the kitchen chair
With chocolate on my fingers, face and hair
3 o'clock my mum came in
She went to put something in the bin.

On the way she came across me
Looking sleepy, sticky and very mucky
She couldn't believe what she saw
'Get cleaned up' she shouted, 'I'll count to four'
I quickly washed my hands and face
Mum shouted, 'Go away! Give me some space!'

I got ever so badly told off
I cleaned the chocolate up with a cloth
She eventually came to forgive me
That's why all you children should see,
Do not pretend to be very ill
Because the same will happen to you, it will!

Danielle Wright (10)
Heartsease Middle School

HOW I FELT

Today I felt really excited
Because . . .
It was my birthday,
But I did not get anything.
I went down to see if there were any cards,
But nothing!
So I went to see if the postman was coming,
But no!
Then I saw everybody getting up.
They all said 'Happy Birthday Aimée!'
Then that was when I was getting really excited.
I thought I was going to get all my presents,
But I did not!
At this moment I was getting really upset,
Because I thought that they had forgotten about my birthday!
I went back down to see if there were any cards
And . . .
There were tonnes of them!
I shouted up the stairs,
'Mum there is a load of cards here!'
Then I got all my birthday stuff,
Then I was really definitely excited!
That night I had a party with all my friends,
That was a good birthday!

Aimée Edwards (10)
Heartsease Middle School

THE THREE BILLY GOATS GRUFF

In a field of grass
Munching and chewing,
Lived Three Billy Goats Gruff.
Nearby a creaking, wobbly, dirty, old bridge,
Underneath welled a stinky, dirty, ragged, old troll.
The little Billy Goat Gruff trotted across with a
Clipperty-clop!
'I'm a troll, foll and roll, and I'd like to gobble you up,'
'Mum's more scrumptious,' the little goat bleated.

Next Mum came over, clippity-clop!
The same thing happened again,
The troll asked his same question
And Mum trotted past.
Then the same thing happened once more,
Then Dad came over, clippity-clop! Clippity-clop!
Dad gave the troll a boot up the bottom,
Troll wet through, scolded by his mother.

Helen Middleton (9)
Heartsease Middle School

THE ALLIGATOR

The alligator is a fierce animal,
A mean animal,
A cruel animal,
The alligator is a terrible animal,
A rude animal,
A not nice animal,
But just make sure
That you don't say it in front of him!

Sarah Snowling (10)
Heartsease Middle School

WITCH'S SPELL

Bubble, bubble,
This is trouble,
Mix with flour,
It will bake in an hour.
Get hedgehog off the road,
There's two of us so get a load,
Get some cats
And some bats,
Mix with spice,
Tip it over your teacher, if she's not nice,
She will turn grey and old after a day,
I'm guessing she's like that anyway,
I am cheeky, I am bad,
It didn't work, I am mad!

Josh Starr (10)
Heartsease Middle School

LAKE BIRD

It flies around the sparkling lake,
With its lovely metallic blue wings,
You can hardly hear this beautiful drake,
But only when it sings.

Passers-by stop and watch her
Sitting on their low deckchairs,
Wondering, does it have fur
Or lovely long, silky hairs?

Leighann Cox (10)
Heartsease Middle School

THREE LITTLE PIGS

In a cosy house, three young ones lived with Ma,
Packing their little suitcases ready to leave,
Mother sighed, 'Find a house of your own!'
The first pig weeping lots, as he packs his bags.
Second pig is happy to leave Mum!
Third pig being lazy and packing slowly.
Their mother packed three lots of hot lunches for them,
They all skipped away.

All went the same way,
First pig saw a friendly man in a field with straw,
Second pig saw an ugly woman with lots of twigs,
Third pig saw a pile of bricks,
All pigs found somewhere and built a house each.
Three different houses were built,
They settled in their cosy homes,
Of straw, twigs and bricks.

Sophie Slatter (9)
Heartsease Middle School

I REALLY HATE THE PARK!

I really hate the park!
Especially when dogs bark!
How people go on,
Are you coming to the park?
But sometimes I really want to go
Then Dad says it's too dark!
It's so unfair!
I wish I could go to the park!

Matthew Asker (10)
Heartsease Middle School

THE BULLY

The bully is tough
The bully is rough
Bully beats you up
Even smash a cup
Over your head,
Call you names
You have to stand up
To the bully,
The bully
The bully
The bully.

Suzanne Breeze (10)
Heartsease Middle School

SNAKES

Slippery skin,
nasty grin,
sharp teeth,
will give you grief,
slithering past,
not very fast,
what will you do
when it bites you?

Aaron Curran (10)
Heartsease Middle School

MR GRUMP

There was a man called Mr Grump
Who did everything in a lump
When he went to the shop
He always blew his top.
He was always feared
Even though he was called weird.
He worked in a mill
Which was on top of a hill,
He worked at night
And got all his jobs right.
He came home at six in the morning
And he always came home yawning
And this is what put him in a grump!

Daniel Seely (11)
Heartsease Middle School

ZOO ANIMALS

Z   igzaggy zebras gallop, gallop, gallop
O   ld and silly otters swim, swim, swim
O   ver the hill you see ostriches hide, hide, hide.

A   ngry animals crunch, crunch, crunch
N   aughty monkeys swing, swing, swing
I   gy the iguana sleeps, sleeps, sleeps
M   ad and mean gorillas scream, scream, scream
A   lly the anteater eats, eats, eats
L   ow the lion yawns, yawns, yawns
S   illy snakes hiss, hiss, hiss.

Stevie Howes (10)
Heartsease Middle School

BUNNY

Although you just sit there all day,
How can that be fun laying in hay?
You used to be funny,
You even liked honey!
Now you're an old hump,
You will never even jump,
You just sit there like an old lump,
I think you deserve to live in a dump!
All you ever do is sleep,
Like an old, messy heap.
I love you,
But you're not new!
So please get up and play!

Kelsey Gooda (10)
Heartsease Middle School

JUNGLE BUG

Once upon a time I met a bug,
He was saying 'Help I'm in a jug,'
He was trying to escape,
With some Sellotape.

It was too sticky
And he went all picky,
He got in a pickle,
He saw a nickel.

He had an idea,
He leapt up with cheer,
He crawled into a tray
And he said 'Hooray!'

Jessica Robinson (9)
Heartsease Middle School

How I Felt

I walked slowly back to my house, tripped
Over a rock and cut my knee.
It was bleeding but it did not bother me.
At that time, all I could think about
Was the school race.
I had come last!
They were too fast!
I was
Nothing
Compared to everyone.
I am so stupid even my brother can beat me
And he is only 3!
I always come last,
I am so silly,
I knew I would
Come last,
I am so silly.

Curtis Pointin (10)
Heartsease Middle School

Monkey

I saw a monkey on a tree
A king bee was coming towards me.
One monkey escaped from the cage,
I asked him 'What was his age?'
He said 'My age is nine,'
That's quite fine.
'Do you want to be friends today?'
'I will be going home on Monday.'

Gavin Marrison (9)
Heartsease Middle School

THE THREE LITTLE PIGS

Three Little Pigs lived with their lovely mother,
They thought they would each make a beautiful home,
One built a house made of straw,
The other, made one of twigs.
The third one made his out of bricks,
They all heard a scary growl,
It's the hungry, dirty wolf,
They all ran for their lives.

Safe in their comfy houses,
The mean wolf angrily knocked on the doors,
'Come out, come out, or I will knock the door down.'
'Not by our squiggley tails we will not let you in.'
Wolf smashed two houses down,
The two pigs dashed to their brother's brick house,
'Come out, come out or I will knock the door down.'
Wolf couldn't smash the house down.

Jordan Wood (10)
Heartsease Middle School

MONKEY

Monkeys swing from the trees
And then they catch a little breeze,
They go up high,
Right into the sky,
They make a bun
And look at the sun,
It hurts their eyes
And then they cry.

Emma Carway (9)
Heartsease Middle School

How I Felt

Every time when it is my birthday,
I am always . . .
Excited and happy!
When I have a sleepover
And I am very, very, very . . .
Excited!
When I see my
Nanny and grandad,
Every Sunday,
I am always excited!
And when I see my mum and dad . . .
I am always excited!

Gabby Timbers (10)
Heartsease Middle School

Me! Me!

It's me, yes me!
I have brown hair.
It's me, yes me!
I have brown eyes.
It's me, yes me!
I have a girlfriend.
It's me, yes me!
I have toys.
It's me, yes me!
I have a best friend, it is Kyle,
It's me, yes me, Jack!

Jack Murphy (9)
Heartsease Middle School

THE GUINEA PIG

I lived on an oil rig
With my pet guinea pig
I went to get it out one day
And it bit my hand away.
It didn't come off,
Until I had a cough.
I put it back in its cage,
To calm down its rage.
The phone rang, it was my auntie from down under,
When she had gone, it started to thunder.
Lightning struck the oil rig
And the cage floated away with that stupid guinea pig.
It washed up in Spain,
Where it started to rain,
Soon it bit someone's nose
And stole all their clothes.
It found an umbrella one day,
Along came a big gust of wind and blew it away,
It landed in France,
Where it learnt how to dance
And danced its life away!

Daniel Ribera (10)
Heartsease Middle School

SNAPPY THE CROC

There was a young croc called Snappy,
Who seemed to be unhappy,
When he cried Mumma,
She smack his bumma
And all he wanted was a nappy.

Kyle Wright (11)
Heartsease Middle School

TIGER

There lives a tiger named Sabrina,
Who lives in Argentina!
She is orange and has black stripes
And she can type.
She has two cubs but they sleep in tubs,
She hunts day and night,
She gives people a fright.
She said, 'Oh no I lost my toe,'
I'd better go and find it.
She found one, it did not fit,
So she looked some more!
But she found a sore,
She said to her husband Ned,
'Have you fed the cub, Ted?'
There was a knock on the cave,
'Hi Mave' said Sabrina,
'You look much meaner!'
'I found this toe in my bedroom drawer,
And lots, lots more!
Sabrina said 'Thanks a lot!
All my toes I now have got.'

Jacqueline Pasco (9)
Heartsease Middle School

A FRIEND

A friend is really funky to have,
A friend is really cool,
A friend is someone to go shopping with,
So that is what you are to me!

Samantha Cox (9)
Heartsease Middle School

How I Felt

Today I feel excited,
I was going on holiday,
My mum was then packing my bag,
But I had no clothes,
I came downstairs and had some breakfast,
Then my mum called me,
'I have found your clothes!'
I got all excited again!
I said, 'Can we go now?'
'Please Mum!'
We got on the plane and went . . .

Lauren Aldis (10)
Heartsease Middle School

The Cat

There was a great big cat,
That wore a massive, fancy hat.
Every morning he had a bath in the sink,
When he got out he gave a big wink,
His fur was so shiny,
With his ears that were tiny.
The cat was chasing some cats,
But he loved eating big bats.
He loved sleeping on soft mats
And he was even afraid of flying gnats.

Olivia Davison-George (9)
Heartsease Middle School

THE HOUSE FIGHT

First my mum and dad,
Then they go mad,
What do I do,
Play the flutes,
Next sister and brother,
Fight with each other,
Auntie and uncle,
Smother each other,
Grandad and nanna,
Play the piano.

Charmaine King (8)
Heartsease Middle School

SCHOOL DAYS

7.30am - time for school
'Mum I've got a headache,' but she's no fool.
'Get up you'll be late for Mr Pool'
'Feel my head, Mum'
'Oh yes it's cool.'

So off I trot,
Like a mule
To that horrible, boring school,
I wonder why Mom's so cruel,
But then again that's the rule.

Kirsha Harding (8)
Heartsease Middle School

CROCODILE

Crocodile, crocodile,
See your mouth and your big teeth,
I don't think you can eat beef.
Your goggily eyes
They are so big,
They look scary to me.
Crocodile, crocodile,
You're big and green and brown and hairy,
Crocodile, crocodile.

Kirsty Anne Burns (9)
Heartsease Middle School

STORM

Storm, storm when were you born?
A long time ago when it was dawn,
Storm, storm what did you see?
Fields, hills and mountains and a beautiful sea.

Storm, storm where will you go?
I'll travel the world and find some snow.
Storm, storm, what will you do?
I'll bring it back to England and sprinkle it on you.

Nathaniel Brian Richard Harper (9)
Heartsease Middle School

THREE LITTLE PIGS

With mother three pigs lived,
Who were now packing their bags,
Mother wanted them to find a house of their own,
Mother was making them two lunches each,
The pigs had finished packing.
One of the pigs was weeping and cuddling Mum.
Another was very lazy who made Mum pack his bags.
The third pig didn't mind at all leaving Mum.

Pigs kissed their mum goodbye,
Glad to go, three pigs slammed the door,
Each walked a separate way down the street.
One of the pigs saw a man in a hut,
He had a lot of straw.
Pig asked, 'Could I have some straw?'
'Enough to build a house please!'
A cosy house of straw he built.

Next pig wanted some sticks,
Saw a man with lots of branches,
He was going to throw them in the river,
Pig asked, 'Could I have some sticks?'
'Enough to build a house please!'
A warm house he built,
Pig loved his new house,
Hardly came out of it.

Michael Hubbard (9)
Heartsease Middle School

POLLUTION

I remember when life was easy,
I could fish with ease
And never have to move nest,
I could eat and drink when I wanted.

I remember when I could swim in fresh water
And have plenty to eat,
I could play and jump and talk,
I had all the time in the world.

Now man have come and
Hunted us and killed the river,
Big, black evil monsters chuck up waste,
Now we must find a new river.

They are killing us those monsters,
We must swim away.

James Nicholls (10)
Kenninghall Primary School

CHRISTMAS

The blades of grass are decorated
Like slithers of glass.
The stars shine sharp and clear,
Like the brilliant cross on the church tower.
Jack Frost running down the garden,
Like a barn owl shooting down in the dark woods.
Children falling down on the slippery ice,
Like skittles scattered in a bowling alley.

Thomas Brown (9)
Kenninghall Primary School

SPACE

A shooting star is bright
Just like a firefly
It's very loud
And sounds like my dad's gun
It goes very fast
It's like a cheetah.

Mars is a red chameleon
Very bright colours up in space
Just like a brick, but not as hard.

Stars are cats' eyes glinting
High up in the sky
As they help light the night
People look and stare.

The stars as bright as yellow snake skin
It's flaming hot like a forest fire,
But its heatwaves are sometimes cruel
It's quite hot and very bright
And it's God's creation, light.

Joshua Bailey (10)
Kenninghall Primary School

I SAW . . .

I saw a squirrel hiding some nuts,
I saw the night swallow the sun,
I saw the bonfire light up the sky,
I saw wild flowers being cut by trimmers.

Torr Cumming (10)
Kenninghall Primary School

A RECIPE FOR DISASTER

Double double, toil and trouble,
Fire burn and cauldron bubble.
A tall giraffe's neck,
A bird that will peck.
The insides of a gnome,
A rotten cup of coffee that's still got its foam.
Two eyes of a cat,
A tail of a rat,
An elephant that will thud
And baboons' blood.
A head of a frog
And a maggot in a log.

Sophie Cumming (9)
Kenninghall Primary School

THE STREAM

I remember when I was clean
But now factories leave fish floating downstream
Making me a deadly stream
Instead of being clean.

I used to enjoy going down hills
And through trees
But now they are killing me
Please, please help me!

Close them down and make me
Clean.

Paul Coomber (11)
Kenninghall Primary School

RECIPE FOR DISASTER

Double double, toil and trouble,
Fire burn and cauldron bubble.
Put in first the guts of snakes,
A snoring troll before it wakes.
Gone off pieces of maggoty cheeses,
An old man when he sneezes,
Add the ashes of a heart,
A beetle living in a mouldy jam tart.
A bloodshot eye of a hundred-year-old dragon,
An inside out elephant on a wagon,
Double double, toil and trouble,
Fire burn and cauldron bubble.
Add a pint of human blood,
A hundred worms wiggling in mud.

Katie Pavid (10)
Kenninghall Primary School

WEST HAM 3 MAN UTD O

Hooray! Hooray! Hooray! West Ham won 3-0 today.
Up against Alex Ferguson's side,
Poor old Fergy nearly cried.

A cracking shot from young Joe Cole,
Through Barthez's legs and in the goal!

The neat shot from Di Canio,
He kicked it hard with lots of flow.

What a save by David James,
The best I've seen in all his games.

Penalty kick by John Moncur,
Passed Barthez with a blur!

What a great match, the West Ham fans say,
While the Man Utd fans are keeping at bay.

Robbie Goodsell (10)
Kenninghall Primary School

THE DEATH OF A SNOWMAN

I watched him all night,
He was white like a polar bear's fur,
He looked magnificent in the dawn light
And then the world began to wake,
The sun came out from behind the moon,
It got warmer and warmer
And then he began to melt,
His hat was the first to go,
His head came down with a lump,
At lunchtime he had only three buttons left
And then he had two
And then he had one
And then he had none.
He was dead.
He had only lasted a day.

Marcus Searle (10)
Kenninghall Primary School

FROST COMES BEFORE CHRISTMAS

The blades of grass are decorated,
　Like slithers of glass.

The stars shine sharp and clean,
　Like diamonds twinkling in the sunlight.

The candle-a-light,
　Like a crystal shining from its cave.

The icicles shining,
　Like snow dripping off a roof to the ground.

Santa going down the chimney,
　Like the freezing wind rapping at the window sill.

The snowman melts in the sunshine,
　Like an ice cube in the oven.

The snow falling from the tree,
　Like a footstep landing on the ground.

The Christmas tree falling over,
　Like Santa slipping on the roof.

Jack Burrows (9)
Kenninghall Primary School

SNOWFLAKES FALL BEFORE WINTER

The glimpse of the sun is like a candle going out,
A snowflake falling is like a fly trapped in a spider's web,
The sparkling snow is like a silver cloud,
The stars are pointed like a thorn,
Hanging brown and bare.

Glenn Stolash (9)
Kenninghall Primary School

FROST COMES BEFORE CHRISTMAS

The blades of grass are jewelled,
  Like glass glowing in the moonlight.
The stars shine sharp and clear,
  Like the bright cross on the church tower.
The snowflakes are falling,
  Like a spider's web.
The trees glittering in the mist,
  Like stars in the night.
The clicking of the reindeer's feet on the roof,
  Like little bells ringing in the church.
The ice on the spider's web glistens,
  Like diamonds in a ring.

Danielle Shaw (9)
Kenninghall Primary School

WEATHER WATCH

Snow falls,
Wind calls,
Icy rivers make no sound,
While wind whistles,
Thunder thuds to the ground,
Snow falls,
Wind calls,
Lightning lights up the town,
Babies cry loudly,
Rain pours down and down,
Snow falls,
Wind calls.

Aaron Grime (10)
Kenninghall Primary School

THE RIVER

I remember when life was good,
Floating down the stream,
Fishes laughing and swimming around,
The goldfish tickled my belly,
I remember making little waves
Everyone having fun,
The frogs jumping on and off my back.

But then things turned bad,
I changed colour,
A week later there were things,
Reflecting on me,
The day's turned dark,
There were fish floating on top of me,
I realised they were dead!

Sophie Fuller (10)
Kenninghall Primary School

FROST

The blades of grass are decorated
Like crystals in the midnight sky.
The stars shine sharp and clear
Like needles on a tree.

The snow on the rooftops
Like a shroud over a statue.
The church bells ringing
Like an alarm clock in the morning.

Summer Copeland (9)
Kenninghall Primary School

WEATHER

The wind soared through the sky,
The wind floated in the air,
The wind crawled round the chimney pot,
The wind glided gently in the air.

The rain fell from the grey clouds,
The rain drifted through the air,
The rain floated round and round in the sky,
The rain glided from up above,
The rain floated from the sky to the ground.

The snow fell on top of the rooftop,
The snow crashed onto the ground,
The snow swept along the floor and
Banged against the trees,
The snow whooshed round the houses
And danced around the cars.

Hayley Brown (10)
Kenninghall Primary School

POLLUTION POEM

(From the river's point of view)

I remember when life was good,
I gossiped to the fish,
We laughed and played together.
But now there are no fish to play with,
I am all alone now,
I've got those awful town shadows towering over me,
I feel really scared.

Laura Turner (9)
Kenninghall Primary School

FROST COMES BEFORE CHRISTMAS

The blades of grass are decorated
Like slithers of glass
The stars shine sharp and clear
Like the brilliant cross on the church tower.

The frost on the trees and frost on houses
Like diamonds through glass
The snowflakes sparkle
Like looking through a crystal ball.

Up above the stars shine
Like looking out of a stained glass window
The clouds look gloomy
Like smoke out of a chimney.

Ashton Flounders (10)
Kenninghall Primary School

POLLUTION

I remember when life was good
And I used to tumble and rumble down hills
I remember when the kingfisher swooped
Down towards me
But now my life has changed and I am miserable
Today a man kicked a can into me
I saw the kingfisher swoop over my head
I haven't seen one lily pad bob over me for ages
Walkers crisps float on me instead
Horror!

Lewis Weatherburn (10)
Kenninghall Primary School

AUTUMN POEM

I saw a leaf falling from the tree,
I saw a conker blast into oblivion,
I saw the grey mist wrap around a tree,
I saw the golden apples fall from a tree,
I saw grass blowing in the wind,
I saw some children with scary faces,
I saw some cats' eyes glowing in the dark,
I saw a man walking his dog,
I saw pumpkins glow in the dark,
I saw a snake slithering on the floor,
I saw some people on a bike ride,
I saw some cows crossing the road.

Ben Garwood (10)
Kenninghall Primary School

THE WIND

The wind soared through the sky,
The thunder fought the lighthouse,
The rain clattered the roofs of houses
And scared the sun away.
The wild wind blew the cars away
And crashed into the houses.
Snow covered houses until they
Were all white.
The hail crashed on the ground.
The howl of the wind,
Soaring through the window.

George Nicholls (9)
Kenninghall Primary School

THE STORM

The wind washed through the sky,
    The wind hunted down its prey.

The cloud moved like a bird,
    The cloud caught a wheezy cough.

The rain screamed through the gutter,
    The rain went clutter, clutter.

The thunder shattered a house and a half,
    The thunder killed a poor calf.

Lewis Knights (10)
Kenninghall Primary School

PARENTS

My nan once said, 'Remember lad,
You must be kind to Mum and Dad:

They do the best they can, poor things:

They work all day, your dad will soon say,
If you don't help you'll get a smack,
Believe me son you don't want a whack.

You'll get another smack, if you keep
Repeating words like that
And believe me you will sleep on the kitchen mat,
They're never wrong, they're always right,
No wonder they can't sleep at night.'

Jenna Clarke-Frary (10)
Mulbarton Middle School

THE LEPRECHAUN

T   he smallest living men,
H   urting nothing,
E   venly spreading seeds.

L   ittle old man,
E   lf-like features,
P   retending to be real,
R   unning around all day,
E   ating mushrooms,
C   hasing off invaders,
H   unting down gold,
A   lways at the end of the rainbow,
U   nderstanding nature,
N   ever underestimate the power of the leprechaun.

Sam Thelwell (12)
Mulbarton Middle School

FIRST DAY BACK

It's the end of half term,
It's first day back at school,
We find out new stuff,
Children are looking cool.

Swimming on Friday,
Children making a fuss,
PE on Monday,
Children arrive on the bus.

Children all clean and neat,
Teachers give out new books,
Children are working hard
And hang their bags on hooks.

Sophie Bland (9)
Mulbarton Middle School

THE MAGIC BOX

I will put in my box,
The greatest show dog on Earth,
The best swimming pool ever
And a special diary with everything in it.

I will put in my box,
A nice lunch box with nice food,
Lots of wishes that were ever dreamed of
And a family with a nice home.

I will put in my box,
A plant in a dog's basket
And a dog in a flower pot
And a nice green plant with leaves.

My box is fashioned,
From gold, pink and silver,
In the sides there are stories
And in the corners there are secrets.

I shall go to a dog show with a dog,
On the biggest party on Earth
And go home and have an ice cream,
With cookies, miss school and walk
Dogs and puppies.

Emma Traynor (9)
Mulbarton Middle School

FIRST DAY BACK

Lunch in the hall,
Lovely smelling food,
Noisy people, nice people too,
Some people are quite rude.

The playground is really big,
Lots of children running round,
I like my new class,
School dinners cost a pound.

Emily Peacock (8)
Mulbarton Middle School

THE MAGIC BOX

I will put in my box,
A world of new things,
A scamper of a dog dashing,
Lush green forest, vast and big.

I will put in my box,
The smile of a class of people,
A celebration of birth,
A whole year round with happiness.

I will put in my box,
An aged birthday of joy,
Easter with eggs for presents,
Christmas of thanks and love.

A fabric silk box,
Designed with sequins on the side,
Decorated with hinges like beckoning fingers,
A golden star in the middle.

I shall learn in my box,
The great crashing waves falling,
All seven wonders of the world,
The fascinating rules of life.

Jessica Ballard (9)
Mulbarton Middle School

MY MAGIC BOX

My magic box is made of
Witches' hair,
A witch's hat and a vampire's cloak.

There are vampires' teeth on the lid,
There are spells in the corners,
The hinges are a panda's finger joints.

I will put in the box,
The broomstick of the most powerful witch
And the zombie that saw light
And a pink diamond from a baby's tear.

I will put in my box the blood of Ann Boleyn
The nose of my gerbil
And the nose ring of a bull.

I will ride a broomstick in my box
And turn myself into a vampire or a witch
And cast spells,
I will create everyone happy and of course,
Evil spells too.

Molly Gallant (9)
Mulbarton Middle School

CATS SLEEP FAT

Fierce, eyed all over,
Getting ready to pounce,
Staring as still as a statue,
Greatly frozen,
Suddenly dives and chases.

Holly Hunter (8)
Mulbarton Middle School

THE MAGIC BOX

I will put in the box,
The lost star, so it will help me all the time,
Coal from a steaming train,
A hare with a hairy tail, with it pointing out.

I will put in the box,
A newborn baby just learning to walk,
The explosion of the world,
A mark of a vampire fang in someone's eye.

I will put in the box,
An aeroplane 3 times faster than the speed of light,
A dog that miaows
And a cat that woofs.

I will put in the box,
A school with children learning
The biggest place in London
And the quickest and fastest train in the world.

My box is fashioned by magic sparks
That make wishes come true,
It has cool and wicked stuff on the magic box
You have to put a code to use it.

I shall be in the biggest football match in the world
I shall score two goals and the crowd is wild
I got hurt and the other player will get the red card
I shall have a go to score another goal and we
Will win! Win!

Jamie Allison (8)
Mulbarton Middle School

THE ADDER

The most infamous land
Predator of the marshes
Is watching his prey.
Peering through the undergrowth,
He picks up the scent on his tongue.
Moving silently over the ground
He watches the mole which is his prey.
Now very close,
He waits
For the perfect moment
To strike then,
Now!
He pounces on his
Unsuspecting prey,
Embracing its neck in his jaws,
Sinking his fangs into its neck.
Half an hour later the adder has
Eaten his fill
And swims in the pool.

Ralph Moore (8)
Mulbarton Middle School

MY MAGIC BOX

My magic box is made of purple fur
And a tiny spark from the moon
And a lock of horse hair and dragon scales
And teeth for stands.

I will put in my box a thousand horses and ponies
And all the animals in the world with
Ten unicorns that can fly.

I will put in my box
The biggest television in the world
And all the chocolate anyone could ever eat.

I will put in my box
A cinema and a piece of chewing gum
That lasts forever.

Abbey King (8)
Mulbarton Middle School

THE MAGIC BOX

I will put in my box,
Some deadly poison from an adder,
Skin of the extinct dodo,
Money from the end of a rainbow.

I will put in the box,
A piece of a ghost,
My best friend Matthew Brighton,
A red electric tooth from an elf.

I will put in my box,
A piece of the core from the middle of the Earth,
The head of a Tyrannosaurus rex,
The whole moon.

My box is old fashioned;
Its hinges are made of a troll's muscles,
It is made of bronze and gold.

In my box I shall swim in the Amazon rainforest
And then I shall fall into a nice warm bath,
Coloured with a rainbow.

Luke Ashby (9)
Mulbarton Middle School

HAPPINESS

Happiness is the sun shining
And looking down from its cool glasses.

Happiness is on the sandy beach
And having a laugh with mates.

Happiness is going on a sunny holiday
And arriving at the posh hotel.

Happiness is being with your family
And setting off on a weekend trip.

Happiness is reading by a red-hot log fire
And rubbing hands together.

Happiness is collecting horse chestnuts
And picking up their spiky shells.

Happiness is when it's bright and sunny
And then it rains and turns refreshing.

Hannah Marriott (8)
Mulbarton Middle School

FIRST DAY BACK

A new classroom or the same classroom
Some teachers new or the same
New shining books which are clean
We all make a good team.

Mothers making a great fuss
Children pulling out their hair
The playground packed with faces
That are about to pop
Teachers crying with despair.

Children bored out of their wits
Children are starting to whine
Children wishing they were in a pit
At last it's home time!

Megan Cletheroe (8)
Mulbarton Middle School

THE MAGIC BOX

I will put in my box,
A dragon that has flames coming
Out of his nostrils,
The music of a bird cheeping
And a super bike doing a wheely.

I will put in my box,
An out-smashing tidal wave
The rumbling of a T-rex
A person shooting a machine-gun.

I will put in my box,
A speedy Dodge Viper
The poison of a cobra slithering
A car doing a skid.

I will put in my box,
A ferocious tiger
The rumbling of an earthquake
Also a Tony Hawkes dark cat skateboard.

I will put in my box,
A PlayStation 2
The world
Also a skeleton of a dinosaur.

Chris Willimott (9)
Mulbarton Middle School

HAPPINESS IS . . .

Happiness is a cloudless sky with
Only the sun to be seen.

Happiness is learning in school
And running around on the playground.

Happiness is playing near the seashore
And buying a lovely ice cream.

Happiness is going into my room
And dancing and singing very loudly.

Happiness is going to the funfair
And going on enjoyable rides.

Happiness is getting on a horse
And going for a quiet ride.

Happiness is drawing a brilliant drawing
And colouring beautifully.

Bethany Wyer (8)
Mulbarton Middle School

MY MAGIC BOX

My magic box is made of gold jewels
It came from the crown of the king of China,
In my box I have a dying witch,
In my box I have a zombie walking through the dead.

In my box I have a remote control car,
It turns into a monster truck.

In my box I have a hundred pythons in a swamp.

Shane Barrett (8)
Mulbarton Middle School

HAPPINESS

Happiness is when Norwich win a match
And when they win 3-0!

Happiness is when Matthew gives me really good ideas.

Happiness is working with Andrew
And playing brilliant maths games.

Happiness is when Millie plays with me,
I love her sweet bark.

Happiness is going into the IT room
And going on the Internet.

Happiness is going to McDonald's
And having strawberry milkshake.

Nick Mackenzie (9)
Mulbarton Middle School

HAPPINESS

Happiness is when I'm at home,
Playing with my puppy because I love her.

Happiness is when I'm at school,
Because I adore maths.

Happiness is when I'm with my family
Because they're the best.

Happiness is when I'm with my dad,
Playing football with him because he's excellent.

Happiness is when I'm at the beach
With my friends because they're great.

Amy Jacobs (8)
Mulbarton Middle School

HAPPINESS

Happiness is when I wait at the bus stop,
When I watch the cars flying past,
Happiness is having an ice cream,
Watching it dripping down my arm,
Happiness is playing a match,
When the mud's splashing up my leg.

Happiness is swimming in the pool,
When it's warm,
Happiness is in school,
Writing a poem,
Happiness is watching TV,
Sitting on the settee,
Happiness is playing with my ball,
On the beach.

Happiness is my cat,
Rubbing around my face,
Happiness is having races,
On the beach.

Jessica Davey (8)
Mulbarton Middle School

STARS

Twinkling and sparkling in the night,
People look up to see you shine bright,
But in the daylight you disappear,
Then in the night you reappear.

There are so many of you way up high,
Does anyone know the reason why?
And why are you yellow and why not green?
It just seems to be the way you are seen.

Why aren't you curved like the sun or moon
Or even like the end of a spoon?
And way up there, not making a sound,
Why don't you come and play around?

Juliette Samson (11)
Mulbarton Middle School

MAKES ME THINK AND SIGH

Like a pair of fleece socks,
A sheep rubbing against me,
Makes me think and sigh.

Like a bare tree with no leaves,
A person with just bones,
Makes me think and sigh.

Like glinting snow on the ground,
A bunch of sparkling jewels,
Makes me think and sigh.

Like a new computer for Christmas,
An electric brain,
Makes me think and sigh.

Like a flickering lantern in the air,
Cars headlights flashing at me,
Makes me think and sigh.

Like weak sun rising,
After spark burning out,
Makes me think and sigh.

Like a clock spinning hour by hour,
A horse and cart wheel,
Makes me think and sigh.

Cayce Curtis (9)
Mulbarton Middle School

HAVE YOU SEEN?

Have you see
A yellow, brown
Or red garden?

Have you see
A green, blue
Or orange person?

Have you seen
A cream, blue
Or green alien?

Have you see
A red, blue
Or yellow dog?

I have seen all these, but I
Don't think you have, have you?

Hayley Jane Parker (10)
Mulbarton Middle School

FIRST DAY BACK

First day back at school today,
There was a look of glee,
Because we were leaving our old school,
The teachers having a cup of tea.

New shoes, new jumper,
Pencil, ruler, rubber,
First day in Middle School,
Makes me just about shudder.

Rebecca Willis (9)
Mulbarton Middle School

THE MAGIC BOX

My magic box is made of fur from a rabbit
And a circle diamond on the lid
It's got brown and green snakeskin on the sides.

In my box I keep Tutankhamun statue
A finger from the oldest lady or man
The toe of a dinosaur
A tail of the ugliest puppy.

In my box I keep the most interesting book
It's got glow in the dark stars on the inside of the lid.

Cherry Meredith (8)
Mulbarton Middle School

A LADY FROM SPAIN

There once was a lady from Spain,
Who was a real big pain,
She went to France,
To learn how to dance
And got stuck in the drain.

She got out of the drain
And went back to Spain,
She told everyone about France,
Where she learnt how to dance
And drove everyone insane.

Louise Stagg (10)
Mulbarton Middle School

THE MERMAID'S DREAM

Below the calming waters,
Where the dolphins play,
A mermaid sits and prays,
That the prince of her dreams,
Will take her away to the
Place where dreams come true.

The mermaid takes a trip to the
Top of the water,
As a ship of gold sails by,
'My prince,' she cries as he
Passes her by,
'Take me away and make my dreams
Come true as we live happily ever after.'

This just goes to prove
That your dreams can come true,
If you wish hard enough.

Simone Self (10)
Mulbarton Middle School

THE RAIN

The rain's been raining all today,
It's soaking and dripping, now we can't play,
It's dampening umbrellas, and soaking the sea,
I am so glad it's not getting me!

The slide is as wet as a river,
The playground is now a great sea,
The weather is not getting better,
I am so glad it's not getting me!

The trees are still dripping and soaking,
The ducks are splashing around,
The lilies and ducks are a-floating
And the poor little frogs nearly drowned!

The rain's been raining all today,
It's dreary and miserable too,
I'm lucky to be dry and inside the warm
And I hope that you are too!

Emma Dudzinski (11)
Mulbarton Middle School

PARENTS

Parents are bossy,
'Do your homework now!'
Parents can be kind,
'Course you can!'
Parents are grumpy,
'Just go to bed and stop annoying me!'
Parents can be annoying,
'Just a minute and don't say but!'
Parents are happy,
'OK darling,'
Parents can be sad,
'Whatever!'

Parents can be,
Bossy, kind, grumpy,
Annoying, happy or sad.

Parents are . . . *parents!*

Rebecca Louise Dye (10)
Mulbarton Middle School

BATH PEARLS

Shiny,
Sitting there,
In a nice white dish,
On the window ledge.
Splash!
In the bath,
Just melting,
Melting,
Melting,
Smell the sweet smell,
Of beautiful pine trees
And sweet smelling roses,
A delicious peach,
All gone,
In a few moments,
I love bath pearls.

Claire Ashby (10)
Mulbarton Middle School

THE BLACK CAT

In the midst of the night,
The black cat pads along the wall,
Suddenly leaping,
Its back arched in a smooth curve,
Landing softly amongst the flowers,
It finds a comfortable place
And sleeps.

Rachel Willis (11)
Mulbarton Middle School

CHRISTMAS POEM

K eeping still,
A t Christmas,
T hanking people for your presents,
H olly on the door,
E veryone is happy,
R ing bells at church,
I nk and bits of wrapping paper,
N uts and chocolate at Christmas,
E ating Christmas dinner.

H appy, smiling faces,
A lways laughing,
L ots of friends for tea,
L ots of people talking.

Katherine Hall (11)
Mulbarton Middle School

FRIENDS

Friends are always there for you,
They will try to make you smile,
If you have a worry or a problem,
They will stay with you for a while.

When you have a friend it is such good fun,
To play games and jump and run,
You can go round each others and sleep over too,
But your best friend will always stand by you.

Bethany Stannard (9)
Mulbarton Middle School

SEASIDE

As the waves come to eat the shore,
The sun floats on its lilo in the sky,
Then the shore asks the sea 'Why?
Why do you collapse on me?'
'Why don't we settle this with a cup of tea.'

As the sea drew in the sand
And shells were left there on the shore,
For me,
For me,
For me,
All the shells to make a necklace,
For me,
For me.

Laura Stephens (9)
Mulbarton Middle School

MY HAMSTER

My hamster rumbles,
My hamster tumbles,
My hamster is cute,
But she doesn't play the flute.
My hamster bites,
My hamster fights,
My hamster is a mess,
But most of all her
House is a smashing
Great thing.

Craig Chadwick (10)
Mulbarton Middle School

A SOARING ROARING ROLLER COASTER RIDE

Rise and rip, dive and dip,
Leaning backwards with the strain,
Rattling, roaring, upwards,
Soaring, swirling, whirling
In your brain.

Looping, lunging, downward,
Plunging, going round a dizzy bend,
Swinging, clinging, heads are ringing,
Holding tightly to a friend.

Hands that clasp, scream and
Gasp, funny feelings deep inside.
Ears are popping, now we're stopping.

That's a roller coaster ride.

Paul Franey (11)
Mulbarton Middle School

MY BROTHER'S DESK

My brother's desk is the messiest thing you have ever seen,
It's like a place you have never been,
Last week I went looking for my book,
So I checked my brother's desk, look!
I found some rats and cats and then the cook.
A moving sandwich, icky or what,
Believe me it was boiling hot,
I found my book next to an old scout,
Now how do I get out?

Liz Bailey (10)
Mulbarton Middle School

FUNFAIR

50 pence to go and ride,
I think I'll sit by my mum's side.

Things that bump,
Things that thump.

Can I go on the coconut throw?
I will go and ask my brother if he wants a go.

People throw high and low, but
It makes you want another go.

Bumper cars go round and round,
They make lots of noise and different sounds.

I like the water chute, splish, splosh, splash,
Mum! I want another go, I'm running out of cash.

Michael Howes (11)
Mulbarton Middle School

CARS

Cars are smashing,
Cars are missing,
Bikes are braking,
Kites are flying,
Cats are fighting,
People are sending,
Kids are rolling,
Fires are spreading,
Volcanoes are erupting.

Sam Catton (10)
Mulbarton Middle School

PEACE

G ood and kind is what we need,
I believe all Earth should be calm,
V iolence is not right,
E verybody deserves peace.

P eace is important in the world,
E arth needs us not to fight over its land,
A ll the wars need to stop,
C oncentrate on giving peace a chance,
E verybody needs peace.

A ll over Earth should have peace,

C hildren are learning bad things,
H aving war is not right,
A ll people should learn to get on,
N obody in the world deserves bad things,
C alling war is a bad thing,
E verybody needs peace!

Jay Baker (11)
Mulbarton Middle School

DOLPHINS

Skin, rubbery and as smooth as can be,
Dolphin so sleek as it swims through the sea,
Long like an arrow, direct as a dart,
Scientists think that the dolphin is smart,
The dolphin has lots of kindness pure,
They'll never hurt you that's for sure.

Charlotte McLean (11)
Mulbarton Middle School

SOUNDS

Zipppp,
Bibbbb,
Honk, honk,
Ratttttle, ratttttle,
Sssssss ssssss
Flussssh flussssh
Woooo woooo
Zooooo
Buzzzzzz
Pikkkkkk
Lickkkkkk

That's what you call sounds
And the biggest noise is
Bang
Bang
Bang!

Cherelle Reeve (9)
St Edmund's Community Foundation School

CHARLIE

C   harlie is my nan's dog,
H   e can behave naughtily,
A   lways barking at us,
R   eady to catch the post,
L   ooking underground from the smell of the lawn,
I   love playing with my nan's dog
E   very day.

Darren Hunter (9)
St Edmund's Community Foundation School

NOISY WORLD

Snakes, lions, cats, bats,
Worms, dogs, also frogs, ribbit, ribbit,
Red ants battling black ants,
Silver shoals,
Swimming on the sea, splash, splash,
Bears are roaring mad, roar, roar,
Bees, wasps collecting honey, buzz, buzz,
Baby rabbit is a bunny, boing, boing,
Some monkeys become very funny, ha, ha,
Humans nick money, ting, ting,
Just like thieves,
Also a ladybird on a leaf, whoosh,
Wow!

Devon Missenden (10)
St Edmund's Community Foundation School

COMPUTER

C omputers are fun,
O n the computer I play games,
M ore adventures I can have,
P eople like them,
U sing them is interesting,
T yping letters to the Queen,
E very day I play on them,
R eading rabbit is my favourite game.

Jessica Horne (7)
St Edmund's Community Foundation School

WATER

W ater sparkling in the sunshine,
A pple bobbing at Hallowe'en,
T rickling like a stream,
E ver running to the sea,
R ivers full of fish swimming.

Charlie Pocock (7)
St Edmund's Community Foundation School

MY CAT

He purrs proudly as he walks into the house,
Then friendly as can be, he walks up and looks at me.

He pounces on my lap and miaows so softly
That he makes himself fall asleep
And then I look at him on my lap and
There is a shining star fast asleep.

Now he's woken up,
Springing with suspicious thoughts,
He timidly, curiously, sniffs around in the yard,
But nothing is to be found.

And then he comes back to me as if
Saying feeding time!
So there I go, I get his messy dish and
Feed him to let him out of his misery
And then he curls up and falls back
Into a deep, warm sleep.

That's my cat!

Sarah Green (9)
St Michael's VA Middle School

THE MAGIC BOX

I will put in the box,
the tide splashing on the bank,
the drops taking the sun and making a rainbow,
the fire from a lethal dragon in flames,
a polar bear roaring at the sun waiting for the next avalanche.

I will put in the box,
the funny laughing from a baby hyena,
the crying of a baby tiger,
the heart of a friendly sabre-toothed tiger.

I will put in the box,
a star flashing across the galaxy waiting for a wish,
the song of a vanishing thrush,
a cry from a laughing baby.

My box is fashioned from the teeth of a sabre-toothed tiger,
the hinges are made of stars covered in rubies.
I shall ride on an Hyenadon through the forest
and through the wavy grass with colours shining in the sun.

Bethany Howard (8)
St Michael's VA Middle School

MOON

Moon,
Moon is a ball,
A silver, rocky ball,
Shining over the surface of the Earth,
Smaller than the sun,
The moonlight ball.

Mohd Afiq Zuber (11)
St Michael's VA Middle School

THE MAGIC BOX

I will put in the box,
the pinks and yellows and purples of the sunset
the swoosh of a wave on the edge of the Sahara desert.

I will put in the box,
the cries of a battle
the myth of the hours monster
the smash of a prize vase.

I will put in my box,
the sound of a church hymn
the scent of a dream feast
the singing of a mermaid which sends you to sleep.

I will put in the box,
the whispering of the autumn trees
the love of my family
the grass-green emerald of a leprechaun.

My box is fashioned in silver and gold
every plant in the world will be woven to make my box
and the hinges are made of love.

I shall hibernate until Christmas and then go back to sleep.

John Chapman (9)
St Michael's VA Middle School

COMING HOME

Smoky Spanish trawler coming in from Africa,
Dashing through the water on a cold and freezing day,
A cargo full of fish, lobsters, crabs and eels,
Coming home to their families and a hot plate of peas.

Bradley Cushing (10)
St Michael's VA Middle School

LOVE

Love the power, as sublime as a flower,
Love is the mesmeric sky, we'll never say goodbye,
Love is my fast beating heart, we'll never, ever part,
The germ, the bacteria of love, fills my soul with hate,
If love really hurts it is only my mate,
I can't bear to think of the damage it can do,
Like a disease, like a terrible flu,
Love isn't like that, it is soft, gentle and kind,
Nothing is sweeter, nothing I find,
I'm devoted to love, as warm as a quilt,
I'm devoted to love, for happiness it was built,
Love will never, ever die,
For in Heaven it flies,
Love with its halo as high as a star,
Love flying above the clouds, flying afar,
Love the power as sublime as a flower,
Love is the mesmeric sky, we'll never say goodbye,
Love is my fast beating heart, we'll never, I say never,
For never we'll part.

Nicole Dyke (9)
St Michael's VA Middle School

THERE ONCE WAS A MAN CALLED JOE

There once was a man called Joe,
Who loved to roll in dough.
He ate some honey,
He always had money
And that is your man
Called Joe.

Josh Cheetham (11)
St Michael's VA Middle School

THE CHRISTMAS SEASON

People rushing about,
People buying presents,
People parking on yellow lines.

People rushing about,
People queuing up,
People writing cards.

People rushing about,
People losing money,
People going mad.

People, people, people
Rushing about.

Leon Bream (9)
St Michael's VA Middle School

OUTDOORS I SEE . . .

Outdoors I see birds twirling, whirling
Through the warm, morning sky
And people walking, talking
And wondering,
Why?
Outdoors I see dogs leap and sleep,
As the wind comforts their ears,
I see a fox hide, by a side
As he waits for some
Deer.

Jordan Scrafton (11)
St Michael's VA Middle School

FOOD AND DRINK

Runny eggs, curry spice,
Sweets and chocolate, very nice,
Pink pork chops, Frosted Flakes,
Cheesy rolls, ready makes.

Coca-Cola, lemonade,
Still water, cherryade,
Orange juice, pink milkshake,
Ice in fizzy, lovely make.

Sausage rolls, coffee, tea,
When you eat onions, people flee,
Rabbit meat, milk and bread,
Eat all these, you're well fed.

Chocs for Mum, beer for Dad,
You drink beer, you're classed bad,
Herbs and plants is what it brings,
Crisps and rolls with cheesy things.

You want food and drink galore,
You keep on wanting more and more!

Hannah Tickle (10)
St Michael's VA Middle School

A SCHOOL LIFE

A school life will always matter,
The teachers say 'Please no chatter,'
Children looking,
Monitors booking,
This is the school life.

Shaun Stubbings (11)
St Michael's VA Middle School

THE MAGIC BOX

I will put in the box,

The splish, splash, smashing,
Of the ocean when tides ebb,
The reds, the ambers, the browns,
The greens and the yellows of an autumn fall.

I will put in the box,

The beautiful black swirling galaxy,
The lovely colours of the world,
A pumping heart of a baby being born.

I will put in the box,

The expression on a child's face
Being silly,
The laughing of my best friends,
The enjoyable people around.

My box is fashioned from
The green nature of the world,
That surrounds me all year round.

I shall listen to the perfect singers,
In my box while looking at the ocean's ebb.

Chelsea Willis (9)
St Michael's VA Middle School

THE WIND

The wind is blowing through the trees,
The kite is flying high,
The young girl fell and grazed her knee
And then began to cry.

The bins are clattering and falling down,
The lids are rolling by,
The rubbish is blowing through the town,
The bin bags in the sky.

Amber Jane Scott (11)
St Michael's VA Middle School

THE MAGIC BOX

I will put in the box,

The stars scattered across the golden galaxy,
The ocean roaring against the beach
And sparkling against the sand.

I will put in the box,

The seagulls zooming across the beach,
The golden sparkle of a rose,
The sharp prickle of a golden shining green holly.

I will put in the box,

Dolphins swimming in the deep blue sea,
Seven colours from the sparkly rainbow,
A flame from the golden sunshine,
My special friend's laughter.

My box is fashioned from

Silver gold steel with a magical star on the top
And little happy faces on the side.

I shall fly with a duck to the moon,
In my box I shall swim across the great Atlantic,
I shall skid down a white mountain.

Gemma Chenery (8)
St Michael's VA Middle School

IS ANYBODY THERE?

Down the narrow, windy lane,
I was walking in the rain
I heard footsteps coming near
My heart seized up full of fear,
I didn't know what to do best
My heart was pounding in my chest
I tried to turn, but full of fear,
Is it footsteps that I hear?
I run and run, but then I fall
Was that my name I heard called?
Someone shouts my name to me,
Oh, it's only Mother, it's time for tea.

Kerri Francis (11)
St Michael's VA Middle School

MY DOG JO

She looks like a panther, dark and sleek,
Ready to pounce up onto her feet,
She crawls like a sniper through the long grass,
She runs like a whippet, ever so fast,
Her eyes are like diamonds, they sparkle at night,
When she got run over, she gave me such a fright,
I'm ever so glad that she's alive,
The vet told us she may not survive,
Her coat is like velvet, soft to the touch,
That's why I love Jo ever so much.

Nicole Kane (10)
St Michael's VA Middle School

THE WRITER OF THIS POEM

The writer of this poem,
Is taller than the Eiffel Tower,
As keen as a student at college,
As handsome as a prince,
As bold as a headline.

As sharp as a knife,
As strong as a diamond,
As tricky as a witch.

As smooth as a cheek,
As quick as a car,
As clean as a hospital floor,
As clever as a scientist.

The writer of this poem
Never ceases to amaze,
She's one in a million billion,
(Or so the poem says).

Amber Diamond King (9)
St Michael's VA Middle School

THE PARK

I went to the park, to eat some bark
I climbed the tree, to kiss a bee
Then I jumped in the pond, just like James Bond
Then I climbed up the swings because I thought I had wings
Then I jumped from the top and did a bellyflop
Then I swung on the bars and I flew to Mars.

Natasha Cranston (11)
St Michael's VA Middle School

MAGIC BOX

I will put in the box,

One hundred silver and gold pearls,
A flame from the sun,
A pot full of magic roses with diamond noses.

I will put in the box,

A rhino racing full speed with magical horns,
My family smiling gently,
Coloured stars shining brightly.

My magic box is made of magical pearls and stars
And its hinges are made out of blue seaweed,
Its lid is made of fairy's hair and the lining is
Made of hard diamonds.

I shall jump into my magic box and go anywhere,
I would go to Africa and ride a cheetah.

Lisa Manning (9)
St Michael's VA Middle School

MY DOG

My dog Barney is so sweet
All he ever does is eat
He's starting to get fat
He can hardly chase the cat
His silky fur is black and white
His short, little legs give him no height,
But he's so warm and loving
When he cuddles me at night.

Emily Bradshaw (11)
St Michael's VA Middle School

THE MAGIC BOX

I will put in the box,

Flashes of lightning, shining like gold pennies,
The twisted spin of spiros,
The sea splashing on the shore.

I will put in the box,

Flames from a dragon's throat,
Stars going past galaxies,
My family smile.

My box is fashioned from
Gold tin with silver stars.

I will ride a woolly mammoth,
In the winter snow.

Joshua Francis (8)
St Michael's VA Middle School

A DOLPHIN

A dolphin splashing in the sea
Having fun just like me.
The sun is sparkling in the sky
And in a second the dolphin says bye.
As I close my eyes and go to sleep
I dream of these creatures of the deep.

Stacey Simmons (10)
St Michael's VA Middle School

MY ACROSTIC POEM

S illy
H elps everyone
A nxious when I have to do a test
N ice
E xcellent at art

B rainy
L augh nearly all the time
A ngry when people call me names
N ot very naughty
C ool
H ates dancing
F unny
L evel two in literacy
O n computer nearly all day
W ants nearly everything
E very day I go out
R ubbish at maths.

Shane Blanchflower (10)
St Michael's VA Middle School

OUR MRS FITT IS...

As purple as a beetroot is her hair,
As funny as a magician,
As sneaky as a mouse,
As cheeky as a monkey,
As chatty as a parrot,
As pale as a moon,
As helpful as a nurse,
As pretty as can be.

That's our Mrs Fitt.

Jasmine Crotch (9)
St Michael's VA Middle School

MY BROTHER

My little brother is five years old
His eyes are blue and his hair is gold
He used to be cute, but now he is old
He wakes me up in the middle of the night
Only because he has given himself a fright
My brother argues
My brother cries
My brother gives me a poke in the eye
I love my brother lots and lots
His smile and laughs
I couldn't live without him
My brother.

Daryl Sparrow (11)
St Michael's VA Middle School

THE MAGIC BOX

I will put in the box,
the autograph of my best friend
a delicious, spicy curry
and my best teddy.

I will put in the box,
my best ice skates
and my nanny's black and white dog
my two stepsisters and one stepbrother.

I shall walk on the damp, shining sand
I will make tall sandcastles
and go to sleep in the sun.

Stanley Winhall (8)
St Michael's VA Middle School

A Dog

A dog barking in the sun, just like me having fun.
Now he's running with his bone to the place he calls home.
Across the fields, road and park, to his front door where it is dark.
The door opens to let him in, to the sound of, 'Where have you been?'

Andrea Lake (10)
St Michael's VA Middle School

The Cat

I'm a fat cat, a mat cat
I'm a home cat, hate to roam cat,
Who likes the brush and comb cat,
I'm a milk cat, life of silk cat,
Who'll never leave his home.

Chloe Brown (8)
St Michael's VA Middle School

There Was A Man Who Liked Peas

There was a man who liked peas
Who also wore dungarees
He met an old woman
Whose clothes were all woollen
And her stripy dog had fleas.

Alison Barfield (11)
St Michael's VA Middle School

MY NAN AND GRANDAD

My nan and grandad are special
They take good care of me
Because when my mum is working
I go round their's for my tea.

My grandad takes me golfing
As we play once a week
And if I've played and beat him
Then he buys me a small treat.

My nanny takes me shopping
And we travel on the bus
Because it is more exciting
As with parking there's a fuss.

And when I sleep at their house
I'm allowed to stay up late
So I think my nan and grandad
Are absolutely *great!*

Jake Roberts (10)
St Michael's VA Middle School

THE CAT

I'm a lap cat
A fat cat
Not a home cat
I love to roam cat
I drink milk cat
I feel like silk.

Amanda Taylor (8)
St Michael's VA Middle School

COLLECTIONS

Fridge magnets are what I gather,
Some 3D, some flat,
I keep them all together,
For people to look at.

Bookmarks, my brother collects,
A box they are in,
Leather is what he selects,
He gets them from places he's been.

Salt and pepper pots, my mum has lots,
Dolphins blue, black and white sheep,
We use the tiger pots,
In the kitchen she keeps.

We have junk in our house and guess whose it is,
Dad's, the junk is,
The junk we would not miss,
So go on Dad, give it a miss.

Leanne Harrison (11)
St Michael's VA Middle School

THE YOUNG WOMAN FROM BUDE

There was a young woman from Bude
Who went to work in the nude
Her manager said,
'You're off your head,'
And she said, 'Don't be so rude.'

James Carter (10)
St Michael's VA Middle School

MY BEST FRIEND

My best friend has long, dark hair,
She's kind with a lovely smile.
My best friend is pretty and smart,
She is the best friend ever, by miles.
My best friend laughs all the time,
She is funny and witty and bright.
My best friend is always with me,
It's like she won't let me out of her sight.
My best friend has a really nice mum,
Who lets me come round for tea.
My best friend is really cool, just you wait and see.

Jocelyn Browne (11)
St Michael's VA Middle School

I AM . . .

I feel like melted snow,
Gone, melted away,
I know I feel so sad inside,
But it's so hard to explain,
I need to find myself again,
I've gone to live in space,
Reality is here no more,
Where's my eyes, my face?
Emotions take over here
In the world where's my part?
I think I now know what I am,
I am a broken heart.

Emily Chapman (11)
St Michael's VA Middle School

DRAGONS

A scorching, horrible beast,
Its jaws are like sharks,
It is so hungry it could have a feast,
It has teeth as sharp as darts.

You better watch out,
Or you'll be next,
Because he can smell you with his snout,
You can send him a nice text.

But he will get you,
For his self,
Before his brother does,
He only wants your health.

Leeroi Smith (9)
St Michael's VA Middle School

MY SISTER

My sister has long, curly, black hair,
My sister is sometimes quiet and sometimes loud,
My sister likes dogs and dinosaurs,
My sister's best friend is Katie,
My sister likes to go to sleep in her warm bed,
My sister is kind and considerate,
My sister is warm and playful,
My sister can sometimes be a monster,
My sister is the best!

Lauren McLaughlan (11)
St Michael's VA Middle School

ACROSTIC POEM

S peedy
P olite
E nergetic
N ice
C aring
E veryone's friend
R eliable

M y mate
O riginal
R espectable
R ight hand man
I ntelligent
S porty
H appy.

Sam Bobbin (11)
St Michael's VA Middle School

THERE WAS ONCE A FISH CALLED BOBBY

There was once a fish called Bobby,
Who lived in a tank in the lobby,
He was there to greet
The people to meet
But swimming was his favourite hobby.

Liam Seaman (10)
St Michael's VA Middle School

SUMMERTIME

S   un is always, always there
U   nder, over, everywhere
M   unching sweets in the sun
M   ums and dads are not much fun
E   nd of day - time for bed
R   est and dream your sleepy head
T   rips you go on and have lots of fun
I   ndeed you have to put up with your mum
M   e and you will play all day
E   nd of day all the fun is packed away.

Stacey Beck (10)
St Michael's VA Middle School

THE DAY I WENT TO SEA

When I was one I had just begun
and I used to suck my thumb
When I was two I was still new
and my mummy gave me a dummy to chew.
When I was three I stopped wearing a nappy
When I was four I could open a door
When I was five I still couldn't drive
When I was six I could pick up sticks
When I was seven, stories were my heaven
When I was eight I could skate
Now I am nine I still feel fine.

Jasmine Malachowski (9)
St Michael's VA Middle School

SNOW

When night flies by
And summer dies
When stars are up above
A rain of snow
Just watch it go!
Flies down just like a dove.

When morning comes
The children run
And play in all that snow
But their toes soon get cold
And the snowman's quite bold,
And they know it'll be there tomorrow.

So as night comes once more,
Winter closes its door
And makes way for spring,
A wonderful thing.

Helen Payne (9)
Saxlingham Primary School

MY WEEPING WILLOW

My weeping willow cries,
And makes all lakes full.
The ducks glide past like fishing boats,
And make a line of bubbles.
My tree looks on the seaweed below,
Swaying its arms as if it knows,
That peaceful times are here to stay.

Hannah Bardsley (8)
Saxlingham Primary School

BOATING LAKE

The boats were bobbing to and fro
Upon the glistening lake,
There was a little, steady breeze,
So there was no need to row,
Ducks were sleeping peacefully
And had no need to wake.

Round the corner came a wherry,
Its mast as big as a thick tree trunk,
The crew all got there by a ferry,
And then away the ferry slunk.

The sun was sinking very slowly,
The lake turned a crimson, deep red,
Some dancing flags were very holy,
And not altogether instead.

Jack Sheldrake (10)
Saxlingham Primary School

TREE HOUSE

A tree is like a person, forever growing,
Forever caring, forever showing
How much space it has to spare
For birds and creatures everywhere.

Take the squirrel for advice,
It thinks its home is very nice,
All because of the tree
Who loves us dearly, do you see?

Elizabeth Bardsley (10)
Saxlingham Primary School

CRYSTAL RIVER

If we have snow,
The crystal river will flow.

What made the crystal river?
I don't think it's the gem snakes that slither.

Maybe we shouldn't be knowing,
That the crystal river is flowing.

But every midnight of the year,
That famous river is crystal clear.

Every second of the day,
The crystal river is blowing gems away.

Some in the ocean, some in the sand,
Some in the open, jungle land.

Never touch the crystal river's way,
Because it will be the last thing you do before your life withers away.

First your fingers turn to ruby, then your body sapphire,
The crystal river is too precious for anyone to die for.

Benjamin Taub (9)
Saxlingham Primary School

THE HEN HARRIER

It swoops and dives to catch its prey,
Skimming the heather along the way.
It's graceful, gliding, silent form,
It cuts through the air at dusk and dawn.
I love the elegant shade of blue,
As it soars above the hills past me and you.

Harry Ewing (9)
Saxlingham Primary School

KING HENRY VIII AND ANNE BOLEYN

King Henry VIII he was quite chubby,
Some people thought he was funny,
He had six wives he liked them a lot,
But still he gave two of them the chop.

But this poem's about Anne Boleyn,
She was very good to him,
Henry thought Anne was nice,
So he took a gamble and rolled the dice.

Of course in the end it turned bad,
Most people thought Henry was mad,
Henry wanted a little boy,
To bring his family pride and joy.

Henry made up dreadful lies,
It would make you gasp with surprise,
Henry said Anne was seeing,
Another male human being.

Most people believed Henry's lie,
Which meant, of course, Anne must die,
Anne was killed with a French sword,
As she died she prayed to the Lord.

George Smith (9)
Saxlingham Primary School

COBRA

Slithering, sliding round and round
Like a carousel,
Opening its mouth to eat an elephant
This is the beautiful cobra.

Kingsley White (8)
Saxlingham Primary School

THE LITTLE KANGAROO AND THE FROG

There was a kangaroo
Who was called Roo,
He lived in Australia
But his jumping was a failure.

He eats leaves and grass
And his coat shines like brass
As he sits in the sun
Having plenty of fun.

His mum came to see
If he was ready for tea
'I'll be home soon
By the light of the moon.'

He jumped off his log
And trod on a frog
The frog gave him a fright
Good job it couldn't bite
Soon they were friends.

James Chadwick (8)
Saxlingham Primary School

THE SNAKE

Slithering line of flesh,
Slimy scales,
Swallowing food whole
Taking weeks to go down the chute,
Poisonous fangs tasting the air with its forked tongue,
Hissing like a balloon being deflated,
Sneaking up to its prey
Then *snap!*

Alfie Chapman (9)
Saxlingham Primary School

THE MOUSE

There was a small house
And in it was a mouse.

He would sit and hold
A glass very cold.

With his feet
On a stool shaped like meat.

His bed he would lay
With his fur very grey.

Him and his friend would always bellow
How nice it was to have a ball so yellow.

Alice Stockton (9)
Saxlingham Primary School

AT 12 O'CLOCK

At 12 o'clock,
When we're all asleep,
Something magical happens around at my feet,
My toys come alive,
Take over the floor and they come into my bed to get
All nice and warm
When suddenly the clock strikes one,
You should see those toys run,
Back to their places where they belong,
Till the midnight hour goes *bong!*

Kimberley Betts (10)
Saxlingham Primary School

NONSENSE WORLD

Nonsense land is silly and very confusing
And when did monkeys lay eggs and chickens eat apples
And cows glide in the air?

Bears lived in trees and hide their fish in hay,
And it rained cats and dogs
People walk on the clouds.

Ducks moonwalked on the grass,
Frogs and toads had teeth
And birds flew sideways
Hatstands grow in the field.

Dogs chased birds in a terrible rage,
Horses bounced around
And snakes could tie themselves in knots.

Joshua Tovée (9)
Saxlingham Primary School

DOGS

Dogs are beautiful creatures
Who like to eat bones,
And lay on their beds
They also like to go for walks
And have a sniff around,
And love to eat scrumptious meat
And lay upon the ground
Dogs are beautiful creatures
With many lovely features.

Freya Lincoln (9)
Saxlingham Primary School

BELLA

I have a pet rabbit called Bella,
And she isn't a little fella,
She is my little baby girl,
To me she's worth a pearl.

Everyone I know likes her,
And every inch of her fur
It's like a great, big, furry coat,
Even though she can't float.

Bella is an English Spot,
She doesn't sleep in a cot,
Her coat is coloured black and white,
She doesn't have one tiny mite.

Her favourite food is hogweed,
I walk her on a black lead,
She lives in the garden, not the house,
She doesn't like a little mouse.

Her best friend is a robin,
She hasn't met a goblin,
She doesn't go to school,
Though she thinks it sounds cool.

My rabbit has a black stripe down her back,
She doesn't have a mac,
Which isn't good
She wouldn't get one if she could.

Sophie Jolliffe (9)
Saxlingham Primary School

HENRY AND HIS WIVES OF SIX

Henry VIII had six pretty wives,
But most of them lost their lives,
Who can forget sweet Anne Boleyn?
She was very good to him.
Their relationship, after marriage, died,
And so did Anne, because Henry lied.
He said she had seen other men,
And she had an affair with them,
For these lies that Henry said,
Anne would have to end up dead,
She was killed with French swords (two not three),
Her head was removed from her body,
Before Anne there was wife number one,
Her name was Catherine Of Aragon,
Luckily she didn't get the chop,
Instead they divorced (Henry told her to hop),
Catherine was sad, believe what I say,
As like one of those things in a soppy play.
Jane Seymour was wife number three,
She died in birth (take it from me),
So here comes wife number four of course,
According to Henry she looked like a horse,
Anne of Cleves was her name (just call her horse)
She also ended up in divorce.
Catherine Howard is the next wife's name,
Her head was removed and she was put to shame.
The last lucky wife was Katherine Parr,
She stayed alive and went very far.

Joshua Smith (11)
Saxlingham Primary School

CUDDLY KITTENS

Cuddly kittens
Have feet like mittens
And snuggle up to your feet,
In the morning they curl up on your sheet.
They jump up and down and spin around,
And play at every sound.

Abigail Burrell (9)
Saxlingham Primary School

PUPPY LOVE

A bundle of fluff lying still on the floor,
A small, wet, black nose shining like a ball,
I call his name, 'Ted, Ted!'
And two beady eyes look up from his bed.
Then all of a sudden that bundle of fluff,
Is doing that pouncy, bouncy, puppy stuff.

Hollie Allison (8)
Saxlingham Primary School

DARKNESS

It's dark and it's creepy
The trees are squeaky,
There are bears growling
Over there.
My friend and I are scared!

Marcus Fenn (9)
Sprowston Middle School

THE BIG GAME

Pass! Pass!
Pass to me
Down the line
I go sprinting

Shoot! Shoot!
Shoot! At me
I might save
The zooming ball

Cross! Cross!
Cross to me!
I flick it
To the ball player

Chip! Chip!
Chip it in the goal,
It's in the net
Goal! We've won!

James Slater (8)
Sprowston Middle School

MORNING

Hooray! Hooray!
It's morning
It's time to go to school,
Time for breakfast,
See my friends.
It's cloudy, but sunny too.

Hooray! Hooray!
It's morning.

Megan Lythgoe (9)
Sprowston Middle School

THE GOAL

I saw the ball
Coming this way
So I controlled it
Then passed again

Then we got a penalty
This boy called Adam took it
And their goalie saved it

Then we got a free kick
Because this boy hacked me
I took it, it whipped
Through the wall and
Went in the goal.
I went 'Yeah!'
And the crowd cheered!

Conor Ferguson (9)
Sprowston Middle School

FRIENDS!

Friends!
Everyone has friends,
Friends!
Even mums and dads
Friends!
Sometimes falling out,
Friends!
Nagging you at times
Friends!

Blaine Kenneally (8)
Sprowston Middle School

MY FRIEND

'Come with me!' I say,
'Let's walk together.'
We talk in whispers, in giggles and laughs.
We smile and sing a tune together
We play silly games and it isn't
Important who wins or comes first.

You are my friend - and we are together.
When I'm sad or moody
You hold my hand.

You always listen and understand
I know you care about me
Because you are my friend,
And we are together
For ever and ever.

Rachael Dixon (9)
Sprowston Middle School

CHOCOLATE

Chocolate
I love chocolate
Sticky, gooey, chocolate
Messy as can be.

I love chocolate
any shape or any size.

I love chocolate
Dairy Milk especially.

Thomas Whitehouse (9)
Sprowston Middle School

BONITA BUNNY

Bonita Bunny is in the wood
Being careful like she should.

Hopping here, hopping there
Bonita Bunny's everywhere.

Bonita Bunny's gone too far
She's dropped her special cookie jar.

Mr Fox, she does not see
Hiding behind a big oak tree.

Bonita Bunny soon falls asleep
Do you know why? She counted sheep.

Mr Fox grabbed Bonita Bunny
Thinking this was very funny.

He laid her on his table and grabbed a knife and fork
Suddenly he sniffed and smelled the smell of black burned pork.

But that gave Bonita Bunny a chance to get free
She grabbed her basket and ran straight past me.

Oh poor Mr Fox, how he missed Bonita Bunny
He'd only invited her in for a coffee!

Freya Riseborough (9)
Sprowston Middle School

FEELING HOT

The sun is hot
Really hot
I want a drink,
But I'm in my cot.
I need a drink
Or I'll turn into ink.

I'm dying of thirst
I think I'm going to burst.
I call for my mum
She comes
I drink my drink
And go back to sleep.

Andrew Godfrey (9)
Sprowston Middle School

WINTER

The wind comes
The sun goes
Winter's here

The clouds wake
The sun sleeps
Winter's here

The leaves fall
Trees are bare
Winter's here

Schools finish
Holiday starts
Winter's here

People shop
People buy
Winter's here

The wind comes
The sun goes
Winter's here.

Louise Daynes (11)
Sprowston Middle School

A Trip To The Fair

Flashing light, shining bright
Loud music thumping,
Thump, thump, thump!
Rides whizzing round and round
And dipping into the ground
Children laughing and screaming.

I could smell the doughnuts in the air
It was a lovely smell at the fair.
Greasy chips, hot dogs and onions
Pink candyfloss like clouds on sticks.

Tired children looking in the air
At the balloons which Daddy won at the fair.
Wishing they could come back
More than once a year.

Taylor Gribben (8)
Sprowston Middle School

The Best Attempt

'Pass to me, I'll shoot to the goal!'

'Pass to me, I'll cross in the ball for sure!'

'Pass to me, I'll shoot it up the field.'

'Pass to me, I'll now try to score . . .'

Goal! Goal! Goal!

Lewis Colman (9)
Sprowston Middle School

HORSE RACE

A swish of a tail
A clop of a hoof,
The horse begins to compete

The rider kicks on
The horse starts to trot,
The competition is carrying on.

Over a jump
Trotting in dressage.
The trophy is in sight
A swish of a tail,
A clop of a hoof
The champion's tournament is won.

Amy Watts (11)
Sprowston Middle School

PHILIP'S MYSTERY CAR

Philip has a new car, but he's sad
because it doesn't go very far.

When he jumps in it to go down town,
he gets upset and angry because it
always breaks down.

When he hops out to see what's wrong,
he realises that the engine's gone!

Then he calls the AA man
and Philip decides to steal the AA van!

Samantha Ellis (9)
Sprowston Middle School

MUM

I have a best friend
    who is always there
When I need her
    who is always there
When I'm in trouble
    she's always there to
Hold my hand to say
    'Don't worry!'
To show me the
    right path in life.
She tries to cheer me up
    when I'm sad.
Angry sometimes when
    I do something wrong.
But makes up quickly and we
    look into each other's eyes.
You've got a friend like mine as well,
    turn round and see . . .
        It's Mum!

Pinku Raja (8)
Sprowston Middle School

RABBITS

They have pointed ears like poles
They hop like kangaroos
Their tails are lovely and bushy
Their claws are like sharp needles
Their furry coats are warm and cosy
Their noses are like wet stones
Their faces are like a cute teddy.

Karlie Aldous (11)
Sprowston Middle School

MY PET

My pet's got no tail, it's also got no legs
and I know you won't believe me, but
it hasn't any arms.
My pet is patterned turquoise and green
and blue, not forgetting red and orange too.
My pet's slippery underneath, with thick
black and white stripes as well.
It has no nose, because it smells
with its tongue.
It can hear through vibrations coming
from the ground.
Can you guess what it is?
Yes of course, it's a . . .
       Snake!

Connor Tooke (8)
Sprowston Middle School

MY BIG DAY

My big day, I run out to play
We stand in a line waiting for
the ball to fly.

The ball's in the air, there's no time to spare,
I run down the pitch to catch the ball,
it's in my hands, I trip and fall.

The other teams are going for a 'try'
I tackled him as he went by,
now is our time to get a 'try'.

I streak down the pitch, running to the line,
I jump in the air, the ball is already there.

Mitchell Turner (9)
Sprowston Middle School

AT THE FAIR

I walk in the gates,
I see the rides
Children scream high and loud.

I sprint to the roller coaster and line up,
Not long now up we go.
We sit in the carriage and the bar falls down,
I get excited.
Here we go!

We go round the corner
We go up the hill
And then zooming down . . .

Suddenly, we break
And I jump off.
I run to see my photo,
Me, smiling and looking up.

Bye-bye fair,
It's time to go,
But I'll come back very soon.

Kirsty Copping (9)
Sprowston Middle School

THE TWINKLING LIGHTS OF SPACE

The sun is light,
The sun is nice,
It shines right through the bright blue sky.
It's one of my friends
Although it ends
It starts in the morning
It starts in the dawning.

The stars twinkle in the dark black sky
The stars twinkle, way up high.
The stars twinkle in the river at night
The stars are very, very bright.

The moon has a smily face,
And it shines all over the place,
Way up in space.

Alix Pudwell (10)
Sprowston Middle School

MY FRIEND

My friend, is my best friend
She goes everywhere with me
We've been to the beach, the park and Sea Life Centre
And when we get back, I make a cup of tea.

I've slept around her house
We've talked all night,
And I met her pet mouse
After six hours we were told to turn off the light.

The next morning, we went skating
We fell over on our bums,
But we said never mind,
Then my friend said 'Let's go home to Mum!'

After that we went to Fatsos,
And we both had fish fingers
And for seconds we had cake
At the end we met some singers.

The best thing about my friend
Is that she's *my* best friend.

Emma Minns (8)
Sprowston Middle School

FOOTBALL

I love playing football
In all kinds of weather,
I kick the ball with my boot
Which is made of leather.

My friends all come to play,
They all think it's a great game,
They wear their shorts and socks,
Their shirts are printed with their name.

I run down the pitch unmarked,
I get the ball and chip
The ball floats toward the goal,
I score! And do a backflip.

My team are pleased we have won,
They shouted my name and are glad
They put their shirts over their heads,
And so do Mum and Dad!

Jamie Steven Brown (10)
Sprowston Middle School

CORFU SUNSET ON THE BEACH

The sun is setting on the beautiful beach,
With a purple, orange, yellow-pink sky.
My feet are sinking into the golden rushing sand.
I love watching the sun go down.

I can smell the delicious aroma of food,
It is coming from the restaurants.
The restaurants are behind a wall
On the lovely beach.
I love seeing the sunset on the seashore.

I hear the clear blue waves flow in and out,
People talking, laughing as well.
Glasses clinking in the restaurants,
I've enjoyed seeing the sun go down.

Emma Lant (9)
Sprowston Middle School

MONSTER

Monsters are scary
Thin and hairy,

Some wear a hat
And some are fat.

Monsters are cuddly
And some are bubbly.

Monsters are strong,
And very long.

Some monsters are small,
And some are tall.

Some are big,
And some are as fat as a pig.

Some are gentle
And some are mental.

Some are muddy,
But they're still my buddy.

Daniel L Knights (9)
Sprowston Middle School

SEASONS

Spring is when there is no fear
when little baby animals are born
like sheep and deer

Summer only comes once a year
when children jump about
and there are no tears

Paddling pools come out to play
filled with water to the top
and there they lay

Colour and light fills the sky
as the clouds pass
and the birds fly by

Next comes autumn, so dull and wet
as the leaves fall to the ground
and the low sun sets

The leaves blow off the trees and fall to the ground
brown yellow and green
there the leaves are found

Winter is the next season which is cold
snow and rain fall
and there it all folds.

Chelsey Ryder (10)
Sprowston Middle School

FOOTBALL

I am on the way in the car
Wanting to see my favourite star,
Out of the window I can see
Small boys with football shirts,
Blowing in the breeze.

Meeting friends, full of cheer,
We down a pint of frothy beer.
Then on we go, to the crowded ground
Where we see the players pound.

We eat chocolate all through the game
Mum got cross and Dad got the blame.
But to help poor Dad, I know what to do
I'll buy some gum, to chew and chew.

The away team commits a foul,
And the home crowd starts to howl.
Our million pound striker, scores a goal,
And jigs around the corner pole.

Our team won, I felt really glad,
So I waved and sang and danced like mad.
Then we walked back to have a Coke,
Laughing all the way, having a joke.

Eleanor Slater (11)
Sprowston Middle School

BEAR

Roaming in the forest deep
Are the animal, we will try to keep.
Catching fish with her big, big paws,
But always following the forest laws.
Through the forest floor she wanders
How to survive this day, she ponders.
And as her cubs fearlessly play,
Mother's never far away.
Dangers never out of reach.
This to her youngsters
She must teach.
She will always do the best she can,
But nothing will save her cubs from
                    Man!

Jenna Wyatt (11)
Sprowston Middle School

THE DEEP DARK NIGHT

There's a deep dark secret
hidden behind the door.
So watch where you're taking
your great big strides.
It might be a ghost,
or even a monster.
So I warn you to stay inside
in the season, called winter.
So what would you do if
a monster jumped out at you?
Would you scream
Or would you freak?

Charlotte Bussey (10)
Sprowston Middle School

BIRDS

Birds fly up high
underneath the cloudy sky.
Over gardens, in trees
high above the bumblebees.
In the shrubs they build their nest
deep inside, safe is best.

Jade Goffin (11)
Sprowston Middle School

NANNY

My nan is a helpful lady,
small or tall, upright or crouching.
With eyes that glisten,
and teeth that shine,
She is my nan, and she is . . .
Fine!

Jenny Andrews (10)
Sprowston Middle School

THE BEACH

At the beach there is a deep blue sea,
colourful shells and slimy seaweed.
Grains of golden sand,
which sparkle in the sun.
It's a great place to go
if you want to have some fun.

Dale Phillips (10)
Sprowston Middle School

SCHOOLDAYS

Schooldays are really fun,
The best days of our lives
First we learn our ABC
Then we're counting 1, 2, 3.

Next, it's learning tables,
Then reading lots of books.
Add, divide and take away,
That's the way we learn today.

In year six we must work hard,
To remember all we've learned.
Soon it will be SATs test time
We'll do our best, it will be fine.

Laura Cossey (11)
Sprowston Middle School

SCHOOL DINNERS

Every day at ten past twelve
We scream and shout for our school dinner,
Pizza, chips, eggs and beans
Every plate must be a winner.

Burgers, sausages and some chicken,
Eat the lot and want some more.
I was thinking of them then,
As I walked out the door.

Stephen Thomas Brown (10)
Sprowston Middle School

KITTEN

She's nothing much but fur
And two round eyes of blue
She has a giant purr
And a tiny midget mew.

A tabby face she has
With four whiskers on each side,
Two pricked ears on top
And a tail that does drop.

She plays in the garden all day long
At night she sleeps in a box,
Which is under the stairs
With my socks.

In the summer she chased my rabbit
Round the garden and tried to grab it,
In the winter she dodges the snow
And tiptoes to where we don't go.

She chases birds in the spring
When she hears them sing.
In autumn she crunches through the leaves
Whilst she's racing round the trees.

I love her dearly
She's my friend
And our friendship will never end.

Gemma French (10)
Sprowston Middle School

THE BEST SCHOOL EVER

The best school ever is right here!
At the school the teachers are the coolest
The head teacher is really nice
The teachers understand your problems
The best school ever is Sprowston Middle School

The best school ever is right here!
Sometimes the teachers are bossy
There are lots of friends to help you
You can have lots of best friends
The best school ever is Sprowston Middle School

The best school ever is right here!
The teachers like cool music
The children are caring
The teachers make you laugh
The best school ever is Sprowston Middle School.

Rebecca MacIntyre (9)
Sprowston Middle School

MONSTERS GO BOO

Monsters are gluey and definitely moody
Monsters are hungry and always greedy
Monsters are spooky, scary and green,
But never mean and glum
But, do they have a mum?

Danielle Clarke (8)
Sprowston Middle School

SWEET LAND

I asked my friend how would you change the world,
'I'll turn the world into sweets' he said.
'I'll have a bed made out of candyfloss
and the world will never be cross
I'll have a TV made out of chocolate
and I'll put sweets in my pocket.
My shoelaces will be made out
of those sweets which look like laces
and I'll have chocolate suitcases.
When I'm sick . . .
my sick will turn into candy sticks
the rain will be chocolate balls and
it will be like shooting a ball in the
football goal!
Yeah! That will be the life for me.'

Roxanne McDowell (10)
Sprowston Middle School

HARRY POTTER

Harry Potter is magical for me,
Fun and exciting for the whole family.
First started as a lonely boy.
Got in trouble all the time,
His relatives thought he crossed the line
Then had a friend to help him through.
Harry became a magical boy,
And wasn't treated like an old toy.

Rebecca Crosswell (10)
Sprowston Middle School

The Night Call

As the darkness of the sky creeps around the garden shed,
Upon my window I can see the stars of light and agility.
The trees blow as a strong gale comes past and they
Go forward and back again.

Never-ending rain comes down, with a pitter-patter, pitter-patter.
As the gale wind storm comes down, clouds are forming all around.

The shadows bounce off the ground, with tall and small,
Long ones on a wet and shabby ground.

A shiver is sent up the back of my spine and as an owl hoots
It must have struck midnight and must be the start of a new day.

Sophie Goldsmith (10)
Sprowston Middle School

Food

F ood keeps us alive
O rganic food is best for us
O ver the world, there are all different kinds of food.
D elicious and lovely are terms of saying

'I like it very much!'
S ugar makes food sweet.

G rapes and other fruit are healthy for you
R aspberries grow wild
E ggs come from all over the world
A pples grow on trees
T angerine is a type of orange.

Laura Cook (10)
Sprowston Middle School

MY MONSTER

My monster is very friendly
My monster sits happily.
The little monster always makes fun
The little monster always sits in the sun.

Some can fight
Some can bite
Some can talk
Some can walk,
Some can joke
Some can choke
Some can smell
Some can tell.

That's all the monsters for today.

Kelsey Cullum (8)
Sprowston Middle School

FOOD

Food is yummy, in your tummy
Also crunchy, but sometimes munchy.

Food is gorgeous, but it is delicious,
But dessert is the best,
Because it comes from the west.

Sponge cake is bubbly,
And jelly is lovely.
But food is yummy,
In your tummy.

Lydia Earl (8)
Sprowston Middle School

MY DOG

My dog was called Penny and belonged to a breed of Cairn terriers,
When we got her, she was tiny.
Her fur would stick up and she was very cheeky,
She would chase her ball all day long,
Gold fluff surrounded her body.
Then as she got older, she became blonder and blonder
Penny became very lazy, and all she would do was sleep.
Sadly on the 31st December 2001, my birthday, she died in peace.
The best thing I remember about my dog was the soft feeling
I would get when I hugged her.

Gemma Abrey (11)
Sprowston Middle School

ON SUMMER'S DAY

On summer's days, my mates and I
Hang out on bridges.
Go to discos
Squash little midges
Eat at Frisco's.

On summer's days, my mates and I
Watch the sun go down.
Fly kites
Buy things in the town,
See lovely sights.

On summer's days, my mates and I
Go to Bedlam's,
Go to the zoo.
Stare at lambs
Enjoy beautiful views.

Becky Holman (8)
Sprowston Middle School

MONSTERS

Monster, monster, green and furry
It will cuddle your teddy.
They live under bridges or in a cave
They might sneak under your bed
So be careful, cos they might say
'Give me sweets, give me rice.
Give me chocolate fudge!'
They have four eyes and they like mice.
He's mad, he's thin, he's gossipy
And he's very, very fat.
He's stinky, shiny and skinny.
He's definitely ugly and big and tall.
He likes eating schools especially
Sprowston Middle and he has
Two noses and five legs.

Laura Louise Earley (9)
Sprowston Middle School

HIDDEN TREASURE

I am the treasure, the treasure, the treasure
Waiting and waiting under the ground.
Waiting and waiting, still and alone,
I could be near, far, high or low.
I could be anything, silver or gold.
I could have been buried years ago.
Nothing like me has ever been found,
Buried in the sea or underground.
Oh, I have a tail and fins too,
I have no claws, but sharp teeth.
A long neck and a sharp beady eye,
Please come find me, find me, find me.

Rachael Sarsby (10)
Woodland View Middle School

VIKING TREASURE

A long time ago when
the Vikings dropped it . . .
It was hidden for a long time.

The Vikings left the treasure
and never came back.
For it's now a sunflower field
Then it was ploughed over
by a tractor.
Now a boy has dug the
treasure up.
It has been discovered
Lovely jewels
encrusted in gold.
The boy has found his dream
Now he is *rich!*

James Beck (9)
Woodland View Middle School

HIDDEN TREASURE

In warm seas under the ocean on rocks
There are beautiful creatures resting.
An oasis amongst the deserts of the ocean floor,
But at night, when the sea is deadly and dark,
The creatures seem to be all alone.
But they are waiting in watery silence for their prey . . .
These hunters are . . .
The Coral Reef
The rainforests of the sea.

Nathan Glenton (10)
Woodland View Middle School

CHOCOLATE TOMB

I had a dog and my friend came round,
We went outside to play,
We played a game of hidden treasure
We looked in the soil and there it was
The treasure map.
Chocolate tomb, chocolate tomb.
We looked in the garden all around,
We went through golden fields full of corn
And deserts full of glistening sand,
Shining in the sunlight.
Chocolate tomb, chocolate tomb
Through seven seas
Into Egypt and there it was . . .
The pyramid of the tomb.
Chocolate tomb, chocolate tomb.
In we went
Through a confusing maze
And even nearly mummified
Chocolate tomb, chocolate tomb.
We won a war
And there we were.
A tomb full of chocolate bars,
Chocolate tomb, chocolate tomb.
We got our bags full of goodies,
And off we went home again.
With our chocolate bars from the chocolate tomb.
Chocolate tomb, chocolate tomb.
Bye, chocolate tomb, bye!

Conor Lake (9)
Woodland View Middle School

HIDDEN TREASURE

Finally it's the weekend,
I can't wait to play.
But first I must mend
My pot, made of clay.
I find it, I fix it
And now I move on.
But what to do next?
I know!
I'll call my friend John.
Over he comes, but what next to do?
We can play with my toys,
That's just what we'll do.
We get to the cupboard and look up and down,
But my favourite toys are nowhere to be found.
We look in the box, the desk and the wardrobe
Where can they be?
Oh no!
I've lost them, but how?
We look in the kitchen, the basement, the bathroom
Still they are nowhere.
Let's go back to my room,
Places where they might be.
Go round in my head,
But then my friend finds them
Under my bed!

Martin Campbell (9)
Woodland View Middle School

HIDDEN TREASURES

People diving under the sea
Exploring sunken ships
Pirates seeking and stealing gold and diamonds
Burying their treasure on desert islands
Hidden from their enemies
Gold and precious metals
Deep beneath the rocks
From years ago
Waiting to be discovered
Lost treasures in pitch-black caves
Rusty, ancient boats
On the dusty seabed
Rubies and silver lost in a deep treacherous cavern
Will these treasures ever be found?

John Taylor (10)
Woodland View Middle School

HIDDEN TREASURE

I am the sparkly, glittering treasure
Hidden in a cave
Underneath a pile of seaweed
Which was thrown into a river.
I am the sparkly, glittering treasure,
Covered in spiky shells.
I contain diamonds which sparkle in the light
Which was hidden by pirates
Which will never be found,
I am the secret, sparkling, glittering treasure.

Laura Dawson (9)
Woodland View Middle School

HIDDEN TREASURE

I am the treasure! I am the treasure!
Waiting to be found.
I've waited here for many years,
Very deep underground.
I am full of rubies
Glistening silver and gold
If somebody finds me
A great secret they will unfold.
I was hidden by a rich man
So nobody would steal me.
I'm starting to feel lonely,
Because there's no one here beside me,
Wait, what's that?
Somebody might discover me,
Maybe even tonight.
Hip hip hooray!
I have been found
I can see the world.
I'm no longer underground,
I am the treasure! I am the treasure!
Finally, I've been found!

Rachel Gaffney (10)
Woodland View Middle School

FEAR

Fear is like a volcano about to erupt,
Fear is the smell of rotting flesh,
Fear is the colour of black,
Fear is the deepest and worst feeling you can have,
Fear lives on the secrets and feelings of others.

Daniel Dack (11)
Woodland View Middle School

HIDDEN TREASURES

Fool's gold, geodes, calcite and rose quartz underground.
Put there before Tudors, Anglo-Saxons and man.
In the rocks they're a pretty sight.
Green, yellow, pink and white.
A ruby holds a red fire.
A sapphire blue, a pale opal and emerald too.
Diamond, as clear as a piece of glass.
Earth's treasures
Once hidden, now found
And now they're on my shelf
Now safe and sound.

Jennie Hudson (9)
Woodland View Middle School

MY TREASURE

My treasure is my mum,
Without her I'd be on the street,
Her beautiful smile.
She does all the housework
And the cooking,
No one can replace her or even come near.
I love my mum so much,
I wouldn't swap her for a million pounds,
She is the most valuable thing in the world,
My mum pays bills, buys me presents,
I don't know what I'd do without her.

Lee Chamberlin (10)
Woodland View Middle School

GOLDEN JEWELLERY

G o on a treasure hunt,
O h what will we find?
L ovely jewellery is what we want,
D own, deep underground,
E veryone is looking for it,
N ow we have looked for years.

J ust look at what we've found,
E veryone is excited,
W ill it be the treasure?
E veryone is shouting.
L et's have a look see,
L ook it really is gold,
E verybody come and look,
R eally, really it is gold,
Y es! Yes! We found it.

Paige Carrigan (10)
Woodland View Middle School

HIDDEN TREASURES

Treasures,
Valuable, sparkly treasures,
You can find them under the sea,
Shiny and glittering.
You can find them in a museum,
Old and dusty.
You can find them underground,
Dirty and muddy.

You can find them in the mine
Dark and gloomy.
You can find them in the mountains,
Cold and chilly.
You can find them in a forest,
Green and glittery.
Waiting and waiting
For someone to find them.

Chris Polley (9)
Woodland View Middle School

HIDDEN TREASURES

H   idden treasures
I   n the cellar
D   own in the dark
D   own in the dust
E   verything is spooky
N   obody's been here for years.

T   here's a gold box
R   ed stars around the sides
E   dged with pretty lace
A   nything could be inside.
S   hould I remove the lid?
U   ndoing the lock
R   eally loud creaking sound
E   verybody's wondering what's within
S   oon all will be revealed.

Emma Cooper (9)
Woodland View Middle School

TREASURES OF THE SEA

Down below
In a sea monster's cave,
Is a chest full of treasure.
I go down into the deep sea.
'Hello,' said a voice.
I looked round.
No one was there!
'Hello,' said the voice again.
Scared and confused
I go on searching for the treasure.
'Hee hee,' it shrieked,
'Who's there?' I ask.
I swim out as fast as I can,
Scared and exhausted,
But the treasure still remains hidden.
I find the cave,
I go in.
'Rahhh . . .'
I see a huge monster
But he looks scared.
I come out of the sea
To get help, but if I tell them
They might kill him.
I will not tell them.
The death of a poor creature
Is not worth a lot of treasure
Because treasures of the sea
Aren't always made of gold.

Siobhan Ivers (10)
Woodland View Middle School

DEEP IN THE GROUND

A long time ago
I saw you
Sitting on the ground
Like a slave
Begging for money
And I helped you out
I gave you a house
I gave you a car
I got you married
And what do you give me
Nothing!
You could have died
But who saved you?
Me!
Because my father helped beggars
And so do I
Because I want to be like him
And be great
And that is it.
But I want to give
You something
This was my father's
And I want to give it to you
This is very special,
It was buried deep in the ground
My father said give this to someone
Who helped me but it only flickers
It's a diamond ruby lighter.

Adam Perry (9)
Woodland View Middle School

MAGIC CHOCOLATE SWEETS

There once was a boy,
Who crawled all around.
He went down the cellar,
And chocolates he found.

Crawling back to his cot,
He climbed straight in,
Eating a sweet,
Something strange did begin.

No longer a baby,
But a man, twenty-one,
And talk he could not,
Which wasn't much fun.

In hiding he taught
Himself how to talk.
And frightened his mum
Who expected a squawk.

The sweets were too nice,
So he ate a lot more,
Being old was a bit of a bore,
So into a baby he turned once more.

Nathan Rowe (10)
Woodland View Middle School

THE MAGICAL SWEETS

There were some hidden magical sweets,
That a boy badly wanted to eat,
He only had two pounds to spend,
And a treasure map he had to mend.
He followed the map to a different land,

He found a dinosaur with a chocolate band,
He asked the dinosaur, 'Where are the sweets?'
The dinosaur pointed to his feet.
On his feet were two big buckets,
Full to the top with chocolate nuggets.

Gary Davies (10)
Woodland View Middle School

HIDDEN TREASURES

Up in the attic I found a map,
It was my nanny's map,
She left it for me before she died,
But nobody knew.
It was really valuable to her,
But I had to find these treasures.
It was in the most unknown place,
Somewhere I'd never thought it would be,
I looked everywhere,
But I didn't look in the cupboard above the stairs,
There it was,
The mysterious thing I had to value,
Right before my eyes.
It was a diary and a photograph,
A very shocking treasure
But it was the greatest,
My nanny wrote a diary,
And now I'm going to continue it.
The photograph was of my nanny.
But the best thing about this was . . .
That nobody knew except my nanny and me!

Laura Burroughs (10)
Woodland View Middle School

MY NIECE

It all began so simply,
A feeling deep inside.
The waiting went on and on,
Like a tree about to blossom.
Then eventually it happened,
The joy held in our arms.
The small face glowing bright,
A face of an angel,
The most beautiful angel on Earth,
With tiny little hands and feet.
Then a pretty little smile,
Happiness filled my heart,
A warm, soft, pink feeling inside,
Tears filled my eyes,
Tears of happiness and hope.
The love I felt between us then
Began to grow
And it will carry on forever
A hidden treasure in my heart.

Laura Boorman (11)
Woodland View Middle School

MY HARMONICA

My grandad left me a harmonica
I sometimes play it,
I sometimes just look at it.
It often makes me sad
But not as much as it used to.
My harmonica is in a box,
I put the box in my drawer.

I can't play it very much
But I can a little.
I love music
I can play the piano, clarinet and recorder.
It is very special
It is my treasure.

Emma Dodds (10)
Woodland View Middle School

HIDDEN TREASURES

There is an island,
A magical one.
It's bright with colours,
There is a cave.
It's dark and gloomy,
Lots of passageways,
Leading to treasure,
Gold, silver and bronze.
There are some diamonds
And sparkling gems.
Hidden away beneath the sand
This treasure will take a clever band
To unearth these jewels.
Which are precious and grand.
There is a creature guarding the treasure,
But what is it?
It roars like a lion,
Jumps like a kangaroo,
Runs like a cheetah,
Has stripes like a zebra,
No one will get past
This creature.

Gemma Kittle (10)
Woodland View Middle School

THE EXTRAORDINARY LAND

A girl was walking in the woods
When she came across a cave,
She walked straight through the entrance
Because this girl was very brave.

She walked up to the dead end
She saw a patch of light,
She pressed on the boulder firmly
And heaved with all her might.

There was a flash of golden sunlight
And dazzling houses of gold,
Even though the sun was out
It was very, very cold.

The castles were made of silver
With sparkling golden moats,
Who'd ever heard of a city
Where it's raining ten pound notes!

The girl walked inside a café
And ordered rice and beef,
The beef was made of diamond
If she ate it she'd break her teeth!

She headed back for home
Thinking of the wonders that she'd seen,
When she got in she shouted loudly
'Guess where I've just been!'

Sam Davison (9)
Woodland View Middle School

GOLDEN TREASURES

Up in the treetops,
High above the ground,
A hut, a chest.

Down on the branches,
Swinging like an ape,
A picture in a diamond case.

Down on the ground,
There's something mind-blowing,
Down in shreds, a map.

In the sea,
Sharks everywhere,
A ship, a notice.

Under the sand,
A sand monster,
In his hand, a photo.

Under the sand and rock
A fire fountain,
A key, a padlock.

Back at my house,
The clues are together,
Will the treasure stay a mystery forever?

Steven Bird (10)
Woodland View Middle School

GOLDEN TREASURE

G olden treasures, find them if you can.
O ther treasures may be better.
L oads of jewels in the chest.
D inosaur bones waiting to be found.
E meralds and diamonds.
N uggets and big blocks of gold.

T reasure, a very, very lucky thing to find.
R eally exciting treasure.
E xcellent treasure, you can't even imagine it.
A lligator bones normally under the sand in the lake.
S apphires shining brightly.
U nder the land a chest to be found.
R emarkable stuff treasure is.
E xtraordinary jewellery.

Tom West (9)
Woodland View Middle School

GOLDEN TREASURE

G one under the sea
O ld chest
L ong, long ago covered in seaweed
D eep down stuck in the sand
E veryone wanted it for themselves
N ever anyone dared to get it until . . .

C helsie once went under the sea
H ad the chest in her hand and looked to see.
E veryone saw a blinding light
S oon she came out with a magic kite
T hat day she flew on the kite around the world.

Chelsie Riley (9)
Woodland View Middle School

SMALL BUT IMPORTANT

My dad carefully brought down a big box from the loft,
It had his mum's things inside.
I blew some dust away, it made me cough
My excitement I could not hide.

My nanny Ann had brooches galore,
I'd love to collect them too,
In a wooden box we found more and more.
Ruby red and topaz blue,
Just looking at them would bring me pleasure,
Glittering, shining little treasures,
The butterfly, parrot, tiger and leaf,
I was so proud I felt I could cry.

To have these brooches was a real treasure
More importantly though, was that each brooch
Represented a part of her life
And I was pleased to be able to see that,
Yes, that is the hidden treasure.

Rachel Wright-Carruthers (11)
Woodland View Middle School

GOLDEN MAGICAL CHOCOLATES

I found a chest under the sea.
I brought it up.
I opened the chest.
I saw golden, magical chocolates.
In the chest there was gold too.
I ate all the chocolates and had good dreams.
I spent all the gold and got good things.

Chelsea Bailey (9)
Woodland View Middle School

HIDDEN TREASURE

One lovely sunny day,
Mum might say why don't you go and play.

Lauren and me went up in the dark, I gasped,
And up there, there was a cross.

So we started to dig, dig, dig,
And so there it was, toys and toys and toys.

And me and her were so amazed,
That we just fell and stared.

Then we saw the bestest thing on Earth,
A photo of our certificate of birth.

And all the treasure we played with all day,
And then we wanted to just have a quick play.

We went to tell our mum.

So off they went to bed
Thinking what an exciting day they had.

Jasmine Fisher (8)
Woodland View Middle School

DIAMOND CHAIN

There was a boy who was walking through the woods.
He walked in, deeper and deeper.
When he came across some goods.
A man had already found them.
He realised it was a chain.
He looked straight into a diamond
And was never seen again.

Benji Moon (10)
Woodland View Middle School

GOLDEN JEWELS

G reat excitement underground, wonder what we'll see?
O n the Earth a girl comes to find
L oads of treasure, maybe.
D own the lane there was a cave, very cold.
E veryone, let's go and see,
N early there.

J ewels, jewels, jewels for everyone, shining, sparkling jewels
E veryone grabbed the jewels and went home
W here shall we go? I wonder what we'll see.
E verywhere we can go
L ovely, we can go to Miami.
S uddenly we're back and it was fun.

Emma Wilcock (9)
Woodland View Middle School

MY MAGICAL CARPET

M any people have tried to find it
A magic carpet hidden somewhere
G o on a treasure hunt
I s it in a forest? Is it in a cave? I don't know
C old, cold caves is where you'll find it.

C ool, we've found it, in a cold cave
A family now has a magic carpet
R eally the carpet does fly
P lease let us keep it Mum
E veryone look what we've found
T oday we will celebrate!

Abbi Finney (10)
Woodland View Middle School

HIDDEN TREASURE

My memories all forgotten . . .
Until one day!
Up into the old, old attic I went and found . . .
A lot of old photos.
It was dark and gloomy
I saw something glistening
So I crept closer and closer
I found a fantastic treasure chest.
I peeped inside
There were lots of things,
A camera with a film,
I ran downstairs to see my mum,
And went to the shops
To have it developed.
They were great photos,
But they were of my nanny and grandad
When they were young.

Lucy Allen (8)
Woodland View Middle School

HIDDEN TREASURES

One day some pirates found a chest.
It had loads of treasure in it.
But they could not open it.
There were lots of padlocks and latches.

What is in it? Nobody knows.
How did they find it? Nobody knows.
What pirates found it? Nobody knows.
Where did they find it? Nobody knows.

Someone tried to open it, they couldn't.
An elephant kicked it, but it didn't open.
People tried to cut the latches, but they couldn't.
Six elephants kicked it, but it didn't open.

Will the pirates ever come back?
Will they ever know what is in it?
Will they ever open it?
Who knows?

Bill Grint (9)
Woodland View Middle School

A HIDDEN NIGHTMARE

Up in the attic
There's a wooden, dusty box.
Open it, open it,
Up the lid comes,
Now it is unconcealed.
There is a blinding light,
Pull it, out it comes,
There it is - a star.
No, it . . . it's an angel.
It has something in its hand,
It's a trinket, oh no,
It's a sword.
Argh . . .
There is silence.
The old room creaks and cries,
In the hollow rotten place.

Amy Dack (10)
Woodland View Middle School

HIDDEN TREASURE

I went in our dark, spooky loft
I saw a big box.
It was shining and glistening
Was it magic or not?
I didn't have a clue!
I crept over to the box
Feeling very worried.
I walked very slowly
I wasn't in a hurry!
I opened the box wide to see what was inside,
I had a look.
There was a big dusty book.
I picked it up.
It was Peter Pan and Captain Hook.
It was brilliant!
I put the book down and them something brown
I saw our ladder so I climbed down!

Dale Rout (8)
Woodland View Middle School

COME AND FIND THE TREASURE

The ships were coming,
The pirate was in trouble,
He had to escape and on the double,
So he sneaked to his cabin,
To grab the treasure,
Then over the side to face the stormy weather.

He swam and swam
Till he could swim no more,
And just in time was washed onto shore
He searched and searched for a suitable plot,

Then drew a map,
With 'X' marking the spot,
Now people have come from far and wide,
But no one can find the treasure he did hide.

Charlotte Stokes (10)
Woodland View Middle School

HIDDEN TREASURE

In the dark and creepy attic
I found a diary with a date on it.
The date on the front was 1962.
The date my sister was born.
In the hospital bed she cried
She really said goodbye!
Her face went bright red
She looked like a burnt piece of bread,
As I looked at my cousin just born.
Until one day he never woke up in the morn
I cried for a day
And never went to play.
Oh, there's the day when Mum and Dad had a crash,
I went into the garden and threw some cash.
It was down to my gran and grandad.
It made me very mad
I tripped over a log.
My grandad was murdered in the woods with his dog
Then my gran had a heart attack
Now it's only me all alone with a blanket,
I wish I could be with them all along,
Where I should be up there with them to be fair.

Lauren Orford (8)
Woodland View Middle School

UNDER THE WATER

Under the water,
I found some treasure,
Here's a cave and more!
Jewels, gems and gold galore,
Up I swam to get a boat,
Down again to fetch the load.

Sapphires blue,
Rubies red,
Crystals clear,
On the sea bed.

Some on stones,
Some under starfish,
Look, a fishes nest,
And what's that glinting down below?
It's gold
I know!

Sapphires blue,
Rubies red,
Crystals clear,
On the sea bed.

I pulled them up,
Onto the boat,
Pull up the anchor,
Push in the oars,
And off we go!

Sapphires blue,
Rubies red,
Crystals clear,
From the sea bed.

Sally Mellows (9)
Woodland View Middle School

SECRET BEAR

I have a bear, a tiny bear,
For no one else to see,
That tiny bear is my secret,
And he belongs to me.

My little bear's a light brown bear,
For no one else to see,
That tiny bear is my secret,
And he belongs to me.

That bear he wears a spotted suit,
For no one else to see,
That tiny bear is my secret,
And he belongs to me.

My bear has soft and silky ears,
For no one else to see,
That tiny bear is my secret,
And he belongs to me.

He wears a ribbon round his neck,
For no one else to see,
That tiny bear is my secret,
And he belongs to me.

My bear he has big, brown felt eyes,
For no one else to see,
That tiny bear is my secret,
And he belongs to me.

And now he's lying in a box,
For no one else to see,
I love that bear, that tiny bear,
'Cause he was made for me.

Amber Kemp (11)
Woodland View Middle School

HIDDEN TREASURES

The deep, dark blue sea
What great secrets sleep underneath the seaweed bed?
While fishes swim by a treasure chest
But no gold, no silver, nothing rare
But an old key lost at sea
Some fishes stop and stare
While others just swim by
But this key rare to whoever lost it
For this key shows love, peace and friendship
Men search for this but never find.

The deep, dark blue sea
What great secrets sleep underneath the seaweed bed?
What use is a key say some people
While others tell the story
Only the fishes know the tale of how, when and why it came to them
For this old rusty battered key
Is not worth anything
But to people living far and wide it is
Is this the key of God?
Only God will know.

The deep, dark blue sea
What great secrets sleep underneath the seaweed bed?
Why was this key sent here?
How, why and when
Only God will know
If God sent it, why?

Why that, why not gold?
Why not silver?
The deep, dark blue sea
What great secrets sleep underneath the seaweed bed?

Alexandra Castle (9)
Woodland View Middle School

MY SPECIAL GIFT

I've got a key ring
As old as can be.
I've got a key ring
With a photo of me.

I've got a key ring
It's the best thing.
I've a key ring
It's purple and green.

I've got a key ring
As old as can be.
I've got a key ring
With a photo of me.

I've got a key ring
It's from Greece.
I've got a key ring
It's the best.

I've got a key ring
As old as can be.
I've got a key ring
It goes with me.

My key ring is a special gift
I take it everywhere
I've never lost it yet
Only once. I left it under my pillow.
I love my key ring
I would never leave it behind.

Jennifer Armes (10)
Woodland View Middle School

HIDDEN TREASURE

On a bright and sunny morning
I was walking on the path.

I was going past a bush,
A book was underneath it
So I took it out.

I went up into the attic
Something hit me on the leg
I thought it was a man hiding
But it was just me!

I started to read it.
It said horrible things
Like I am going to beat him up.
The floor creaked
It was the floorboards,
I screamed 'Help!'

Tom Edwards (9)
Woodland View Middle School

SURPRISE INSIDE

Inside a door
On the floor,
Something special,
Better than metal,
A jewellery box,
With lots of locks.

I look around
Then on the ground
What do I see?
A big, shiny key
Will it fit?
Mmm, will it open it?

It turns with a click
And my heart beats quick,
And inside
Rings, but beside,
All shiny and gold
And very, very old,
A pair of earrings.

Natalie Steer (11)
Woodland View Middle School

HIDDEN TREASURES

At the time of the Salem witch trials
There was a witch called Willow.
She was named after her mother's favourite plant.
But Willow had to go to the wood
With her friends and enchant nature.

Someone found out that they were witches
And told other people.
Willow and her friends were going to be decapitated
Willow hid her spells, books, a small packet of herbs
And her hazel wand under the ground.

In the year 2012
Two girls found the hidden coffin
And started a coven to perform spells.
Their coven started to grow
They were very successful.

To some people witchcraft isn't real,
But there are others
Who think it's fun,
But to Willow it was her life,
And they were her hidden treasures.

Evie Warren (10)
Woodland View Middle School

HIDDEN TREASURES

A treasure more precious,
Then diamonds or gems,
No one, or nobody,
To take it away.

A feeling that's there,
A fire inside me,
A ray of sunshine,
That never burns out.

It does not need much,
But it is better than toys,
It does not run out
And it stays forever.

This treasure I keep,
Is safe in my soul,
It's my treasure
And its name is
Happiness.

Jennifer Crothers (10)
Woodland View Middle School

HIDDEN TREASURES

Peace is happiness
Happiness is health
Health is life's greatest treasure
The greatest treasure is life

Love is loyalty
Loyalty is laughter
Laughter is joy
Joy is a ray of hope
One of life's greatest treasures

Freedom is happiness
Happiness is friends
Friends are family
Family is my greatest treasure.

Connor Metcalf (11)
Woodland View Middle School

TOY SEAL

I've got a soft, cuddly seal
I found it in Spain.
I cuddle it when I'm alone and upset.
In Spain I got soaking wet
So I sheltered the seal
From the rain.

It's as soft as a pillow
And as cuddly as a baby
It is small and white
I love my seal
And I will never leave it behind.

I can't wait until night
So I can cuddle up with my seal
So I can cuddle it really tight
And eventually fall asleep.

I think my seal is a special gift
Just for me,
No one else,
My seal is really cute.

Anna Watts (10)
Woodland View Middle School

THE EVERLASTING CHOCOLATE

There was a boy called Jimmy Summer
Who went to the village raffle.
He won a chocolate bar
It wasn't much of a prize.
He liked chocolate
So he took a bite and said,
'It was good!'
Was it good because it was magical?
It was magical because it kept on coming back.
He didn't show anyone
And for the rest of the year he had chocolate.
For his breakfast, lunch and dinner.
After a year the spell was worn-out
And he ate all of the chocolate bar.
After that he never wanted to eat chocolate again.

Jake Pointer (10)
Woodland View Middle School

AFRICAN MAN

In the cabinet, an African man
Carved out of a block of wood.
He stands, on guard with club and shield,
He keeps an eye on all who pass by.
His tall headdress
And his twisting snake-like necklace,
The pointed bone piercing his nose
Makes him a grand warrior,
I see him at night
It gives me a fright
Because it's a scary sight.

Adam Page (11)
Woodland View Middle School

BRUNO, MY TEDDY BEAR

I can't sleep
It's so unfair
I really miss
My teddy bear.

Where can he be?
He was here yesterday,
But where did he go?
I need to know.

He's brown
With dark black eyes,
If you see him
You'll know he's mine.

I feel so empty
I need him now,
Or I won't sleep
Until he's found.

He's not in my room
I've looked everywhere,
Upstairs, downstairs, left and right,
He's just nowhere in sight.

One more look
I want him now,
I look under the stairs
And there he is
My Bruno the bear.

My eyes are gleaming
With delight
As I take him upstairs to bed
Night, night!

Georgia Long (10)
Woodland View Middle School

HIDDEN TREASURES

Walking through the silent park,
Hidden treasure of peace in my heart,
Hiding every shade of unhappiness,
As I scour the wilderness:
Shrubbery, animals,
All the birds a-flutter.
As a rabbit hurries by,
A treasure with no key,
An egg, catches my eye.
Happiness spreads from my heart,
Warming my body.
Taking it to my den,
I make a nest
Of earth and branch,
Then carrying it home to warm with a bulb.
I long to experience new life.
That day at last comes to me
And when I see the crack,
Joy glows in my heart,
As the beak pokes out -
I know this bird is my hidden treasure.

Richard Castle (11)
Woodland View Middle School

THE CLOCK

It ticks all day and all night
The pretty clock on the right
The pretty clock that belongs to me
The pretty clock with the key.

The pretty clock is brown and gold
It's delicate and very old
When I need to wake up quick
I set my little tick, tick, tick.

With my clock I feel so great
I feel so great because it's my mate
If I lose it I need it found
I really need it around.

My antique clock is my dearest possession
My great grandad had it in 1907
It's special to me
My tick, tick clock with the golden key.

Victoria Reeve (11)
Woodland View Middle School

MY HIDDEN TREASURE

My hidden treasure is golden,
But of no expense.
My hidden treasure is priceless,
But everyone has it.
My hidden treasure may be deep, deep down,
But may be seen all around.
My hidden treasure is soft and gentle,
But it may be sentimental.
My hidden treasure is showing that you care,
Even though others may laugh and stare.
My hidden treasure is good to have,
But sometimes people think it's not.
My hidden treasure is sometimes hard to show,
But most people will never know.
My hidden treasure is like Mother Nature,
It will go on forever after.
My hidden treasure is kindness,
Kindness can never be lost.

Matthew Moon (12)
Woodland View Middle School

HIDDEN TREASURE

As I crept up the attic stairs
I looked right and left to make sure nobody was there.
In the attic there was something shiny like a key
I slowly slid up to the thing and then I stared.
I got confidence to go up to the dusty lid of the wooden chest.
I looked inside. It was full of treasure.
There were whistles and books and a broomstick.
I moved things about in it,
Old stuffing from the toys and creepy-crawlies.
It was very dark and dim,
Something moved and out jumped . . . Jim . . . my dog,
How he got in there I don't know.

Grace Edwards (9)
Woodland View Middle School

MEDALS

Football is the best sport ever
Well it is to me.
And to win a medal, a real medal
Is such a golden treasure.
I'm good at football
Some might say
But some might say I'm not.
I know inside I am quite good
Whatever people say
I have some medals, some real medals
And I treat them with pleasure,
And to have some medals,
Some real medals is such a golden treasure!

Christopher Riley (11)
Woodland View Middle School

MY OLD TIGER TEDDY

My old tiger teddy, he's really kind of battered
His tag is very tattered.
Most of the time on my bed he lies.
He's very small,
But he's very cool.
He cuddles up with me in bed
His name is Scratch.
He's as cuddly as can be.
His fur is soft,
He sleeps with his tiger friends in my bed.
His tail is long,
He's orange and black.
He's mine to keep
Forever and ever,
My old tiger teddy.

Daniel Grint (10)
Woodland View Middle School

THE PLECTRUM

It's a key to unlock the music of the guitar
A magical instrument, a heart of fire, like an animal.
As the drummer beats on his drum
The guitar sings the notes of Hell,
The plectrum is a key to immortality,
The plectrum is special to me.
My father gave me his,
I treasure it, but it is a key to something else,
The music of the world.

Thomas Ryall (11)
Woodland View Middle School

MONEY BOX

It is a hidden secret
And that's how I want to keep it.
My money box is special to me
For no one else must ever see.

I've had it since I was one year old
And I dreamt that it was real gold.
For no one else must ever see it,
Because I want to keep it a secret.

Its colour is ruby red
And I hide it under my bed,
I lock it with a silver key
My money box is safe as can be.

When I take money from my box
I am as sly as a fox,
I like to hide my treasures there,
That I never ever want to share.

Kelly Smith (11)
Woodland View Middle School

THE KEY TO MY TREASURE

I've got a dark secret,
That no one else can know,
But when the word slips,
Then my dark secret will show.
But you have to feel high,
Like a mountain in the sky
And hope for the best
That someone won't slip to the rest.

Some people just can't be trusted,
No matter how loyal they are,
But if they do tell,
Then they're to be distrusted.
Some people can keep secrets,
Some people can't at all,
But if they find that hidden treasure,
Then try to trust them all.

Charlotte Morgan (11)
Woodland View Middle School

A SQUIRREL'S HIDDEN TREASURE!

Squirrels running, having fun,
Singing from the gentle woodland breeze,
Birds chirping in the sun,
But one little squirrel is trying to find his keys.

Trying to find the keys to his secret room,
The room that holds his nuts,
If anyone finds it he's at his doom
And he'll be locked inside their huts.

He'll be made the other squirrel's slave,
He'll have to wash, clean and scrub,
He'll have to live inside a cave,
He'll be made to live with a bear cub.

The other squirrels can't know,
Because outside, no more nuts are left,
Some day he'll have to show,
Otherwise he's committed theft.

Emily Stephens (11)
Woodland View Middle School

HIDDEN TREASURE

As I slowly crept into the dark, gloomy attic
I saw a dusty box in front of me.

I heard a creak, I rushed towards the box,
It was just the old floorboard.

I opened the box, a photo of me,
Me tripping over, I remember that.

Oh, a book or should I say a diary,
I opened it, oh look, it says '19th January, went to beach'.

I remember that too,
That was a very good day at the beach.
Memories.

William Grant (9)
Woodland View Middle School

HIDDEN TREASURE

When I was in the shed
I found a metal detector.

I went and got my dad
And got a box down and another.

I found an old box
That looked like a treasure box
But it wasn't!

That night I dreamed all about treasure.
It was all gold jewellery.
There were watches, necklaces,
Rings and golden coins.

Louis Tidswell (9)
Woodland View Middle School

HIDDEN TREASURE

I was walking along the old, damp street
There was not a peep from anywhere.
I saw an old house, in I went.
I went upstairs in the old house,
It was so creepy I didn't make a sound.
I went in the attic and there was a china doll
And a big, big bowl,
It had a big blue rim.
I was so amazed
There was a diary, it told a story,
I went a bit further and there was a big cupboard,
There was a very funny picture
With a family having fun in the sun.

Natalie Owen (8)
Woodland View Middle School

HIDDEN TREASURE

I moved into a haunted house
It was scary!
I found a secret doorway
It was pitch-black.
I saw something shiny
I went down there
It was scary!
There were cobwebs,
There were old dolls,
There were rocking horses,
There were old photos,
There was one with my grandad on.
They are good memories.

Shona Watling (8)
Woodland View Middle School

HIDDEN TREASURE

I crept up to the attic
There was a couple of boxes.

There were photos in there
They look like my mummy and daddy
When they were little.

The next time I went
To look in other boxes.

I see a chest
But I can't open it.

I found a key
It fitted the lock.
There was nothing in there.

Andrew Walpole (8)
Woodland View Middle School

HIDDEN TREASURE

My ship was sailing across the sea.
The ship hit a rock,
The boat began to sink, I dived into the sea.
I went under the water,
I saw a brown thing,
I went down to it,
It was a treasure box.
I opened it,
I was very happy,
I felt I was king of the world.
I was king!

James Bennett (9)
Woodland View Middle School

MY PHOTOGRAPH

My mum and dad have split up
So I've a photo of them which isn't to be seen.
I never have felt the same
But they are still good friends.
It was the 1st of February when they split up
I have never experienced anything worse.
Mum was so stressed when it all happened
Dad was upset.
The photo was taken on holiday in 2000
We went to Mallorca.
We were a family
Now we're just separated.
This photo is one of the whole family
My mum, dad, brother and me.

Sophie Betts (11)
Woodland View Middle School

THE MAN WHO MADE A DIFFERENCE

My treasure is a person
His heart is ever growing
He is a lonely person,
But he has made a difference
In his spare time he gives out help
He isn't very rich
He works for the RSPCA and more!
He as taught everybody a lesson
That money isn't everything
You can help, rich or poor,
Support is what everybody can give.

Edward Allison (10)
Woodland View Middle School

A VERY DEEP SECRET!

I have a very special secret
And I haven't revealed it yet.
I've kept it for months and years
And I won't ever tell it, I bet.

I keep getting butterflies,
Because it's so hard to explain,
My heart keeps on thudding,
Again and again.

Every day I go outside
And listen to the birds singing,
I try to get it out of my head,
But the secret keeps on ringing.

I've tried very hard
And tried my best.
I'm not ready to tell,
My secret yet.

Siobhan Allen (10)
Woodland View Middle School

HIDDEN TREASURE

In the dark room
Standing among the chairs
I saw a weaving loom
Under the stairs.

The room smelt dusty
The floor was rusty
Hidden in the cupboard
Was an old board.

In the cupboard
There was a chest
Covered with a cloth.
A chest of sparkling,
Precious gold and rubies.

Jazmine Harmes (8)
Woodland View Middle School

BOOKWORM

I've got a hidden treasure
That fills my heart with joy.
But every time I'm at school,
It tries to slip out!

Its doing my head in,
It's a very big secret.
People will just laugh
And make fun of my secret.

I think of it every night,
But it's still there.
I dream of it every night,
Every night in my ingenious dreams.

I've got to let it out!
Here we go.
I've really got to tell you,
I'm a great big bookworm!

The books just open up a new life,
Jacqueline Wilson, Roal Dahl, poetry books.
It's like another world!
Really, I advise you to
Read!

Elizabeth Dewsbury (11)
Woodland View Middle School

A SECRET

In the world there's more than one secret being hidden,
The only thing I used to have, was a secret being hidden.
Everyone in the world must have a secret being hidden,
In a safe in your mind there's a secret being hidden.
Did you get it from your best friend?
The secret being hidden, when did you get it?
The secret being hidden, where did you keep it?
The secret being hidden, no one knows.

Are you going to tell anyone about the secret,
Because I won't tell about the secret,
So no one will know!

Emmaleigh Webb (10)
Woodland View Middle School

LUCKY PENNY

I walked along the road one day
To find a friend who wanted to play.
I came across a ginger cat
And said, 'Hello' that made it scat.
I carried on up a hill
And then I met a boy called Will.
He was very busy and carried on,
I wondered where he had come from.
Then I saw a shiny thing, what was it?
I picked it up and had to sit
I was happy with what I'd found,
It was only a penny not a pound.
But see a penny, pick it up
And all the day you'll have good luck.

Geoffrey Bunting (10)
Woodland View Middle School

BASEBALL

On the shelf
The smell of leather
Is where I keep my special treasure.
Black and brown is its colour,
It fits my hand really tight
And comes with an odd shaped ball!
It travelled far on a plane
My dad brought it home from New York.
I don't play with it much
I want to keep it as it was bought.
When I dust my bedroom
I often pick it up
And pretend to be playing a proper match
The game isn't played much in England because . . .
My special treasure is a baseball glove and ball.

Phillip Fordham (11)
Woodland View Middle School

PICTURES OF DOLPHINS

I love dolphins,
They're speedy and streamline.
They spend lots of time looking for fish
And when they jump they splash and splish.
They're in warm water like Spain
And sometimes in the polar seas,
They live in pods of about 1000.
I know all this from a special book of dolphins
And my favourite picture is a mum and calf.
On holiday I hope to see some in Majorca.

Emily Dixon (10)
Woodland View Middle School

DEEP FEELINGS

Let's go on a trip to a treasure island
Making our way up to the highland
To try to find our feelings
Deep down inside
Let's release our dark eerie feelings
And our dark, deep nightmares true.

We made it up to the top of the hill
And the fish had to be grilled
While the crew were singing through
I was making a horseshoe
Using a screw, nail and bamboo
Whilst seeing a kangaroo.

Yesterday he found it,
He found his deepest feelings.
We tried our best
And left the rest
And now it's gone forever.

The future's only starting for him
Now the dark feelings are gone
We're wishing ours away
In the darkness of the day
So help us try
To make them die
So they are gone forever.

Matthew Plane (10)
Woodland View Middle School

PROMISE NOT TO TELL!

I have a deep, dark secret,
That will blow your eyeballs out of your sockets.
I promised myself I wouldn't tell,
But I might overlook that rule,
If you promise not to tell!

My deep, dark secret,
Means a lot to me!
I've told all my friends
And I might tell you,
If you promise not to tell!

This deep, dark secret,
Is hidden in my heart.
It might be happy, it might be sad,
But you will find out,
If you promise not to tell.

My deep, dark secret,
I am going to tell,
A few of my friends know
And you will know,
If you promise not to tell!

Yes my deep, dark secret,
Is that I love my family
And I hope you do too!
But now you know you must,
Promise not to tell!

My family are my hidden treasures!

Adam White (11)
Woodland View Middle School

HIDDEN TREASURES

Hidden treasures are deep down below
In your heart where it glows
Hidden treasures are your own
Not to share but to keep to yourself.

Hidden treasures are far away dreams
Fantasies in distant places
Hidden treasures can be secrets
Hidden in your heart, locked away.

Hidden treasures can be anything
From deep dark desires to sweets and chocolate
Hidden treasures are your own
Locked away in your heart!

Hazel Pointer (10)
Woodland View Middle School

HIDDEN TREASURE

I'm going on a holiday
And it's gonna be far away
When I'm on this holiday
I'll see the sun every day.

I'll go to the beach and eat a peach
When I'm at the beach
I'll get everyone an ice cream each.

I'll make a sandcastle
And meet a mongrel
I'll find some treasure
With lots of pleasure
Isn't that a hidden treasure.

Adam Stagg (11)
Woodland View Middle School

BOB THE COP

Bob wanted to be a cop,
His favourite food is cod,
He became a cop in New York,
His second favourite food is pork.

There was a robbery in Washington DC,
He looked for ID on his PC,
His name was Al,
But he had a pistol.

He escaped to Atlanta,
Along with his pet manta,
Bob said, 'My god this is cold!
Hey look I've found some gold!'

Peter Berryman (10)
Woodland View Middle School

THE TEMPLE

I am on a mission,
To a mystic tomb,
Far away near my doom.
My heart is thumping,
Yet I am excited,
An *Aztec* tomb I fear,
Is near.

As I pull away the twigs and vines,
Birds and animals sing in line.
I see a golden spear of light,
I walk towards the shining light,
The *Aztec temple* spoke of fright.

Jordan Hare (10)
Woodland View Middle School

SECRET DESIRE

I cannot see you
But I know you are there
You stare at me as you walk by
Nobody wants to talk to me
But all I want is a friend.

I cannot speak to you
But you must listen to me
My heart is burning for a friend
Because inside me you will find
Something very special.

My mind is here and I feel your presence
But inside me there are feelings
Only one can uncover.

As the sunshine shines on me
I think maybe one day I will find
A friend who understands.

Charlotte Leeming (11)
Woodland View Middle School

I HAVE GOT A SECRET

I have a secret
That no one can see
You cannot see him
For he is make-believe.

He lives behind the sofa
He has teeth like a gofer
He eats only loaves of bread
He has ears which are bright red.

He has flaming orange hair
He did it for a dare
His teddy bear
Is called Blair.

I saw him in bright yellow flares
Sliding down the stairs
But I do not care what he wears
He is still my best friend.

Leanne Finch (10)
Woodland View Middle School

PEOPLE'S TREASURE

A treasure to someone can be,
Secrets deep inside,
A treasure to someone can be,
Love which has to hide.

A treasure to someone can be,
Scenery and art,
A treasure to someone can be,
Something straight from the heart.

A treasure to someone can be,
A first tooth or hair,
A treasure to someone can be,
Love, freedom and care.

A treasure to someone can be,
Angels flying high,
A treasure to someone can be,
Dreams and honesty.

Josh Carrigan (11)
Woodland View Middle School

HIDDEN TREASURES

The sky, all year, is a hidden treasure.
If people would only take the time to look up to the heavens.
The colours of day, the sun's golden light, a gift to Earth,
Forgotten by humans, but giving us sight.
Evening comes, sunset begins.
The shades of the sky's dreams are what we see:
The purple, the red, the blue and dying yellow
Slowly giving way to the sky's sleep.
Best of all I cherish the night.
The moon and all her children,
Unnoticed by Earth's people as she sits and watches us.
Even in a storm when the sky is angry, the beauty I see is there,
As the sky roars out his fury and shows us ribbons of dangerous light.
I smile and watch his temper.
Though the sky is never hidden, who is aware?
I am the only one who looks to see.

Danielle Cawdron (11)
Woodland View Middle School

MY CUDDLY TOY

I've had this cuddly toy
Since I was born,
So it means a lot to me.
He's there for me
Through the good and bad
And he's there when I am sad.
My little blue teddy
I'll treasure him forever.

Kel Haywood (10)
Woodland View Middle School

HIDDEN TREASURE TO ME IS . . .

Hidden treasure to me is my family being around,
Hidden treasure to me is an egg with a tiny life inside.
Hidden treasure to me is peace and love in families everywhere,
Hidden treasure to me is secrets I know my friends will keep.

Hidden treasure to me is a dream I know that I will love,
Hidden treasure to me is a shell I found at the beach.
Hidden treasure to me is a feeling of knowing that sometimes I'm safe,
Hidden treasure to me is a book I really enjoy.

Hidden treasure to me is laughter with my friends,
Hidden treasure to me is having a roof over my head.
Hidden treasure to me is a sunbeam upon my face,
Hidden treasure to me is . . . *life*.

Amy Cooke (11)
Woodland View Middle School

THE SECRET OF ORE

The new Trade Federation has been made
Ore processors are chomping ore like dragons
The ore is short and needed for tec level three
With the food collected The Trade Federation reach tec three
The fortress is built and the workers on ore carry on.
Now the fortress is built and the Nova processors are working.
The Nova provides the destroyer Droids with a little help from carbon.
The shining glow of green nova fills the dull sky
The protocol Droids carry the carbon back to the carbon processor.
The processor upgrades to horn beedrill carbon collectors.

Jack Taylor (10)
Woodland View Middle School

HIDDEN EVIL POWERS

This is how it began
With a girl called Linda Locket
She had a leather jacket
With a brass button on the pocket.

The jacket was very weird
She wore it just at night
She tried to stay unnoticed
For she gave people quite a fright.

People could never work out why
All the things she wore were black
She even wore black glasses
With a black cape on her back.

But one day it all went wrong
And Linda started to change
She'd lost her leather jacket
And things began to turn strange.

It was all very clear now
She never went near fire
She always wore black
It was because she was a *vampire!*

Karl Curson (11)
Woodland View Middle School

HIDDEN TREASURE

My hidden treasure is the pleasure,
I find in everyday,
From all my friends and family,
Especially my nanny.

More words could not describe,
Without you by my side,
The feelings of real emptiness,
As each night passes by!

Deanne Fulcher (11)
Woodland View Middle School

BABY ANGEL

Swept away from us before the age of two,
My dearest sister I never had the chance to know you.
You have gone to be an angel,
I hope to join you one day.
You are a hidden treasure though not one that hides.
You are always there inside my head
You are always visiting me through my dreams,
Bending over me to kiss my forehead,
I wake as I see you fly with your angel wings right back to Heaven.
Where you were stolen from us to live in Heaven for all eternity,
When your life was stolen from your lips.
You are my only hidden treasure.
It is a secret why you left me and my family
Don't you agree it is not fair on you or me?
You are like a beautiful rainbow,
One that always stands brighter than the day before.
You are a sun setting over my heart,
You are an angel to me and always will be.
I would give my life to spend one day with you
Then to spend my entire lifetime without seeing you once.
Swept away from us before the age of two,
My dearest sister I never had the chance to know.

Lynsey South (11)
Woodland View Middle School

HIDDEN TREASURE

Hidden treasure is happiness, watching a child smile and be happy,
Hidden treasure is joy, having another human being in your life,
Hidden treasure is a hidden talent, just waiting to meet new people,
Hidden treasure is patience, to help young and needy children,
Hidden treasure is respect to a person who you like, hate or love,
Hidden treasure is saying goodbye to a long loved family member
who is important to you,
Hidden treasure is a secret that has been kept for a long time
which you don't want to tell to anyone,
Hidden treasure is a gift to you given by a special person or a
best friend,
Hidden treasure is a time capsule waiting to be found beneath
the surface,
Hidden treasure is honesty, being able to know they don't lie,
Hidden treasure is trust, tell a secret which you know they will keep
for you,
Hidden treasure is peace, no wars or terrorist attacks like
September 11th which caused devastation,
Hidden treasure is kindness to others, like your best friends or enemies,
Hidden treasure is friendship, no bullying to people you don't like,
Hidden treasure is happiness, watching a child smile and be happy.

Charlotte Harper (11)
Woodland View Middle School

SOMETHING SPECIAL

Hidden treasures are not pirates and chests of gold,
But something small or secrets untold,
Perhaps a shell, tooth or a toy,
All things special to a girl or boy,
It could be families, love or friends,
A deep feeling that never ends.

A hidden treasure is also peace,
When all wars and fighting cease,
Another one is happiness, no fighting and goodwill,
A hidden treasure could be something as simple as a shell.

Cara Oxbury (11)
Woodland View Middle School

HIDDEN TREASURES

A person I once knew,
Had a treasure that grew and grew,
Which they cherished with all their soul,
But in turn diminishing all their hope,
In love, life and play.
He left us in sadness,
That's how he lives his life today.

A person I once knew,
Had a treasure which grew and grew,
His passion for work, fitness and health,
This caused our security to falter,
So we saw the brutal truth.

The person I once knew,
Before we saw the web of truth,
Was someone uncorrupted,
Who could love with all his heart.
He could make the sun shine on a rainy day,
And could make you laugh and play.

His vision became clouded,
And he stumbled off the edge,
He had a hidden treasure,
Just locked up . . . inside.

Elspeth Clayton (12)
Woodland View Middle School

HIDDEN TREASURE

Hidden treasure can be a hundred things -
A man with good luck
A child with a shell
A flower growing wild
And not yet picked -
All these are hidden treasures.
A night full of stars
Filling me with joy
A roaring lion
Free in the wild
All these are hidden treasures.
A memory of someone gone
Thoughts of shared moments
Old toys in the attic
Special family photos
All these are hidden treasures.

Laura Brancalion (11)
Woodland View Middle School

TREASURE

T   reasure is life in a tiny egg,
R   ight in your heart is a treasure,
E   ssential to you is your treasure,
A   treasure is special to you,
S   pace is a treasure to see,
U   nder you is a treasure
R   ight here and now you have a treasure,
E   nvelope your treasure and keep it safe.

Joe Robinson (11)
Woodland View Middle Schoo

My Treasure

The love I get when I see my mum is happiness,
She gives me love in a bright way.
The kindness and happiness she brings,
Make my dreams come true.

My mum is great to me,
Sunbeams come through the clouds with her.
She cares and shares her love,
She gives me space and freedom.

Mum is my treasure, she brought me here,
I have a good life because of her.
Her smiles and kisses
Are the greatest treasures of all.

Theo Chamberlin (12)
Woodland View Middle School

What Is Hidden Treasure?

What is hidden treasure?
Is it some gold or silver?
Is it something you treasure but someone else doesn't?
Is hidden treasure something buried with someone who died?
Is hidden treasure something someone doesn't know about?
What is hidden treasure?
Hidden treasure can be anything.
It could be anything you treasure.

David Stagg (12)
Woodland View Middle School

My Discovery

I walk along the blustery, blowy beach,
Looking down to see what I can find.
Hidden treasure can be anywhere,
In the sky, below the sea, the love of a sister, the trust of a friend,
Maybe even the protection of an animal.
My toes start to get wet,
The water is coming, trickling up my feet,
Then slides back to the cold sea,
Leaving behind my famous treasure,
A living thing inside,
Tickling my hand.
My treasure is now my secret.
Trudging through the sand, I place my treasure,
Back into the flowing water,
Where it floats away, swimming below the welcoming sea.

Lauren Elliott (11)
Woodland View Middle School

Past, Present And Future

I have a gift,
But not a curse.
I see tomorrow,
Past, present and future.

I've seen my wife,
My one true love.
I feel that she
Came from above.

I've seen my life,
In just one night.
This gift from God,
Is not a curse.

This hidden treasure,
Which is mine,
Is used at night,
But not at will.

Scott Berryman (12)
Woodland View Middle School

HIDDEN TREASURE

H   idden treasure
I   ce, frozen on the ground and gleaming,
D   oves, joining until one parts.
D   reams, spinning in my mind
E   verybody here.
N   ight-time, pitch-black and dark.

T   houghts glimmering in my mind,
R   aging fires, dancing and sparkling,
E   very moon and sunbeam like a falling angel,
A   tree in full bloom,
S   unsets, down on the beach,
U   nder the shining stars at night,
R   ainbows, all colours thrown in,
E   verything that lives.

Luke Goffin (11)
Woodland View Middle School

MY HIDDEN TALENT

There it goes again, the school bell,
For another boring half hour of football,
But I don't play, I wander around the pitch.
Bored, dejected, frustrated, annoyed, left out.

Then the ball comes my way, it's heading for the window,
I jump, I catch it, I save it from the window,
My hidden talent is out.
Fantastic, great, marvellous, excellent.

I was given a trial in goal for the team,
Will I save? Will I let them down?
First shot easy, saved to my left.
Relief, comfort, assurance, ease.

Second shot, a catch, third shot, a short dive,
Forth shot, tipped round the post,
When our defender brings the striker down in the box.
Nervous, anxious, tension, pressure.

A last minute penalty to keep us in the cup,
Where will the striker put it?
Left, I dive left, I save it. Full time 0-0.
Exuberant, joy, happiness, excellent, brilliant.

Joe Wilcock (11)
Woodland View Middle School

MY HIDDEN BROTHER

I am on a journey,
And I'm hoping to find,
One special relative,
That's been left behind.

I don't know if they're male,
Or they could even be female,
I have been all over England,
But nothing has prevailed.

I need to find my relative,
Honest I really do,
I need to find my relative,
But I don't know what to do.

I now know where my relative is,
And I will go and find him,
And I found out that he's male,
And his name is Joseph Tim.

I have found my long-lost brother,
And he gives me lots of pleasure,
I have had fun all the way,
He is my hidden treasure.

Craig Acheson (11)
Woodland View Middle School

MY BEST FRIEND

My best friend is someone in my family,
I admire and cherish her,
We're like Siamese twins, stuck together,
I love it when I see her,
My cheeks go rosy red.

I just can't wait for that cuddle and kiss,
Before I go to bed,
In the morning breakfast is there,
Waiting on the table.

Me and her have a friendship plate,
It means so much to us,
If we feel ill, frightened or angry,
We remember those words,
Which makes us feel loads better.

Everyone says we're like each other,
Pleasant, polite, generous and nice,
Maybe that's why we share the same birthday,
People know we have this special thing,
It's called love,
Love is what we have and always will have.

Charlotte Ling (12)
Woodland View Middle School

HIDDEN TREASURES

Splashing through the rocky pools
The sun is hot
The water's cool
My toes curl around a frayed, old rope
I'll follow it
Then wait and hope.
At the end there's an old wooden box
I break it open with some rocks
I lift the lid, look inside
And shining back to my surprise
Is sparkling treasure
That hurts my eyes
Gold and diamonds
That twinkle and shine
As I found them
I think they are mine
The clouds start to roll by
I hear my parents shout and cry
They call my name
I'd better hurry
What about my treasure?
I start to worry
The sun goes in
The sparkle of my treasure starts to dim
I look inside my wonderful box
All I see is stones and rocks
It must be magic treasure
For all to see
As long as the sun is shining
On the sand and sea
I pick out a special stone
To take home with me.

Thomas Semmence (9)
Woodland View Middle School